D0064910

CRIMINAL JUSTICE PLANNING

Administration of Justice Series
   Harry W. More, Jr., Series Editor

CONTEMPORARY CRIMINAL JUSTICE
Harry W. More, Jr. and Richard Chang
Editors, San Jose State University

EFFECTIVE POLICE ADMINISTRATION:
a behavioral approach
Harry W. More, Jr., Editor,
San Jose State University

CRIMINAL JUSTICE PLANNING:
a practical approach
Michael E. O'Neill, Ronald F. Bykowski and Robert S. Blair

THE CHANGING POLICE ROLE:
new dimensions and new issues
Roy R. Roberg
University of Nebraska

EFFECTIVE POLICE SUPERVISION:
a behavioral approach
George T. Felkenes
University of Alabama in Birmingham

CRIMINAL JUSTICE PLANNING

a practical approach

O'Neill
Bykowski
Blair

JUSTICE SYSTEMS DEVELOPMENT, INC.
SAN JOSE, CALIFORNIA

© 1976, by Justice Systems Development, Inc.

All rights reserved. Published 1976.

ISBN: 0-914526-02-2

Library of Congress Catalog Card Number: 75-40692

Published by
Justice Systems Development, Inc.
P.O. Box 23884
San Jose, California 95153

Printed in the United States of America

Contents

Preface

The Criminal Justice Planning process is probably the most misunderstood process in the field. The lack of a general body of knowledge in criminal justice planning would attest to that fact. This text is designed to bring together the bits and pieces of criminal justice planning into a logical, practical and useable framework. Hopefully, this framework will be useful to the student and practitioner in criminal justice. The real test of the usefullness will be the judgments from the students and practitioners alike.

The outline of the text follows what the authors believe to be a logical sequencing of planning activities. Where appropriate, a resource section has been added at the end of selected chapters as a means of providing practical examples that clarify and illustrate specific planning techniques. We believe the text fills a current void in criminal justice literature and will serve as an impetus for further exploration by students and practitioners.

The authors would like to give special thanks to Dr. Harry More, San Jose State University, for his encouragement and suggestions in developing this text. Also, we would like to extend our deepest appreciation to Dr. Kenneth Mayall, Evaluation Specialist, Office of Criminal Justice Planning, Region M, Monterey, California, who spent countless hours reviewing and critiquing our drafts.

MEO
RFB
RSB

Chapter Objectives

1. Historically derives the beginning of criminal justice planning.
2. Develops trends for the future directions of criminal justice planning.
3. Implys that criminal justice planning is an emerging profession formulating its way toward establishment and acceptance.
4. Develops the criminal justice system as a set of processes linked together by the offender.
5. Defines the elements and missions of the components of the criminal justice system.
6. Establishes the need for criminal justice planning.
7. Describes the benefits of planning.
8. Briefly describes the process and steps which form the planning process.
9. Differentiates between the different types of plans.

1

Introduction to Criminal Justice Planning

As one begins the study of criminal justice planning it is immediately apparent that this is a recently created process and consequently is in its evolutionary stages. Even the concept that the criminal justice system is a system is challenged; and the concept that it is a series of processes linked together by the offender is set forth in this chapter. Each of the processes is described in terms of its mission. The need for criminal justice planning is established as the link that brings the individual processes of the criminal justice system together in such a manner as to harmonize the diverse individual efforts. The benefits of planning are described, as well as the process and steps to be used in criminal justice planning. The chapter concludes with a discussion differentiating between the different types of plans and how they relate to the planning process.

The Emergence of Criminal Justice Planning

A decade ago phrases such as "criminal justice planning" or "crime-oriented planning" did not exist in the vocabulary of public officials. Few police, courts and corrections agencies articulated what was desirable for their own agency, let alone what should be worked for in conjunction with other agencies.

In 1967, the President's Commission on Law Enforcement and Administration of Justice recommended that in every state and every city an agency of one or more officials should be specifically responsible for planning in crime prevention and control and encouraging their implementation. The recommendations of the President's Crime Commission reflected a concern for systemwide planning. This meant at the very least ad hoc coordination among police, courts, and corrections agencies so that policies implemented in one part of the system would not have an adverse effect on other components.

The creation of state and local criminal justice planning agencies and departments under the Omnibus Crime Control and Safe Streets Act of 1968 has given criminal justice planning a systemwide focus. The National Advisory Commission on Criminal Justice Standards and Goals encourages the development of criminal justice planning efforts and of allied governmental efforts that contribute to the planning process such as program budgeting, intergovernmental emphasis on evaluation, measurement of government performance, and construction of integrated information systems.

Planning is becoming more than a concern over processing efficiency. It is becoming impact-oriented. Restrictions in the costs, fear and harm caused by crime are being planned for directly. A more sophisticated, long range type of planning is now slowly being achieved. In addition, planning efforts are coinciding with the spread of program budgeting (budgeting by objectives) which, like planning, is future oriented. Finally, recent federal, state and local funding of integrated information systems appears likely to give planners the data-base they lack at present. Increased emphasis on performance measurement will be a probable result of the more abundant flow of information. Planners will be engaged heavily in the design and the use of evaluation efforts.

None of the developments described above are advancing evenly in each state or unit of local government. Yet these are national trends that cannot be ignored. The emerging criminal justice planner is the spearhead for these trends as he simultaneously creates and defines a new profession in the annals of the evolving criminal justice system.

The Non-System System

The current operation of the criminal justice system in the United States has not been successful in the prevention and control of crime. This failure is primarily due to a criminal justice system that attempts to decrease criminal behavior through a wide variety of uncoordinated and sometimes uncomplimentary efforts. The key components of the criminal justice system—the police, the judiciary, correctional institutions, and community based social agencies—have varying degrees of responsibility for removing the causes of crime. These system components have responded to the current crime situation without sufficient understanding of their mutual responsibilities and common objectives.

This lack of understanding is manifested by the failure of each system component to take part in joint planning and action, and also by friction, conflict and deficient communication. These failures result in ineffective crime prevention and control and inefficient resource utilization.

For example, the role of law enforcement is to arrest suspected offenders—their performance is partially judged by the number of arrests they make. They are not publicly judged on the quality of their arrests, rather the quantity. Therefore, if a law enforcement agency becomes over-zealous in its arrest efforts, sight may be lost of the necessary evidence required to develop a good case resulting in a valid conviction. A common complaint voiced by prosecutors is the poor quality of case reports they receive from the police, thus making convictions almost impossible.

The prosecutor on the other hand is partially judged publicly by his success in obtaining convictions. On the other hand, a public defender or defense attorney is judged by his success in getting suspected offender's charges dropped. Nowhere in this adversary process is either the prosecutor or defense judged publicly by his ability to apply justice. Rather this is assumed to be part of the professional ethics associated with the personalities and character of these criminal justice system employees.

The courts carry the torch of being individuals—thus sentencing offenders as they see fit as opposed to operating under a code of uniform sentencing policies. A court in one part of a county may give an offender a suspended sentence and 90 days probation for a minor marijuana possession charge while another court in the same county will decree a year in the county jail as its sentence for the same charge.

Corrections personnel are torn between the philosophies of punishment and rehabilitation and wind up performing neither with any degree of success. They are further burdened with over-crowded conditions in antiquated facilities. Community based corrections, an emerging offspring of the rehabilitation philosophy, is striving to prove its concepts. These constitute but a few of the frictions, conflicts and miscoordinations that are representative of the criminal justice system. It is precisely these diverse interests, objectives and turmoils that the planner must somehow harmonize in a directed effort for the reduction of crime.

Criminal Justice System Defined

The criminal justice system as defined for the planning model in this text consist of four basic elements. The first element and the largest in population and scope (in fact the originator of the remaining elements of the system) is the society or environment which the system serves. Within this society, which is usually a county in structure, are the sub-elements: the crime victim, offender and the formal criminal justice system including police, courts, corrections and private agencies.

Figure I-1 pictorially displays this concept of the criminal justice system. Within the boundaries of a given society, a law violation takes place. The output of this violation is usually a victim and an offender. Sometimes, as in the case of victimless crimes, the offender and victim are one and the same.

System Component Missions

The police are responsible for the maintenance of social order within the constitutional and ethical restrictions set by the society. As illustrated in the following (Eastman, 1969, p. 3) the mission generally includes:

- Preventing crime through the maintenance of order, controlling situations which could result in conflict, and discouraging anti-social behavior.

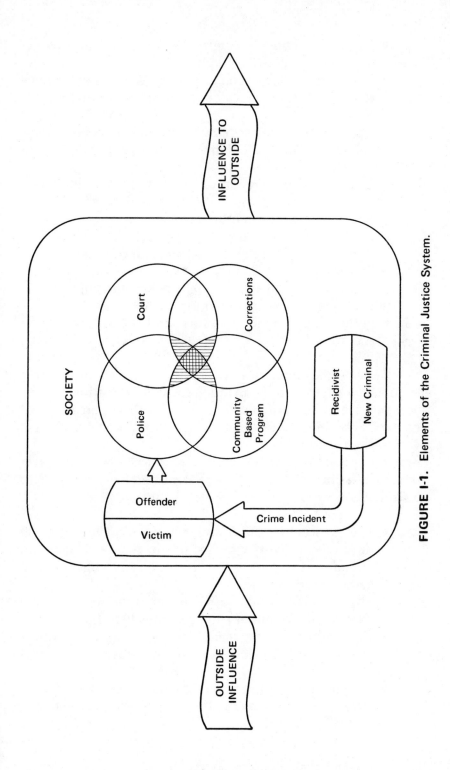

FIGURE I-1. Elements of the Criminal Justice System.

- Repressing crime through adequate patrol and reducing opportunities for criminal behavior.
- Detecting crime as soon as possible after its occurrence (either through direct observation or a citizen complaint).
- Apprehending offenders as quickly as possible enabling the punishment and rehabilitation of those convicted.
- Recovering property in order to reduce the monetary cost of crime and lessen opportunity for criminals and others to benefit from the gains of crime.
- Regulating noncriminal conduct through activities such as enforcing traffic and sanitary code provisions.
- Performing miscellaneous services peripheral to basic police duties such as search and rescue operations, licensing, operating detention facilities, etc.
- Performing public relations and public education activities.

The specific methods and operations used to satisfy these responsibilities vary in individual societies according to the local policies of law enforcement officials, their perception of their role, the interest of elected officials and social pressures within the community.

The courts subsystem serves as a focal point or pivot upon which the criminal justice system revolves. The court's duties include:

- The prosecutors office and/or the Grand Jury making the decision as to whether to file charges against an offender. This process includes the investigation and gathering of evidence.
- The judiciary (plus juries as appropriate) deciding whether the offender shall be convicted of a crime.
- The judiciary, with the advice of corrections, determining what is to be done with the offender after conviction.
- Providing defense counsel to indigent defendents.
- Determining which offender may be released on bail or own recognizance.

- Performing appellate review and decision making.
- Providing check and balance upon the executive agencies such as the police and other local government departments.
- Performing both criminal and civil prosecution, judicial and defense functions.

Briefly, the court subsystem seeks conviction of the guilty and freeing of the innocent.

The chief prosecutor and judicial seats within a given society are usually elective. Thus their methods and operations are (theoretically) responsive to the surrounding social structure.

Within state court systems there is frequent jurisdictional overlap and confusion somewhat similar to that present among municipal and county police departments and county sheriff's agencies. The current state of disorganization within the police and court components does much to frustrate the interrelationship between the two.

As we stated previously, the goals of each element of the system differ. Police define success by the number of arrests, the prosecutor defines success by the number of convictions, the public defender considers himself successful when he frees an accused offender and the courts have taken it upon themselves to use the interpretation of laws as a means of legislation.

Police are accused of improper evidence-gathering, giving poor testimony and overly harassing parolees. Similarly, the courts are charged with dismissing too many cases because of minor technicalities. As a result the interface between the courts and police is hindered by disorganization and lack of communication.

Following adjudication and sentencing, convicted offenders may either be fined, committed to jail, placed on probation, sentenced to the state correctional institutions or given some combination of these penalties. Most of these possible results involve the correctional process, in attempting to prevent future criminal acts by rehabilitating convicted offenders. It is a fragmented process, occurring at both the state and local levels involving both correctional facilities and community supervision, and under the jurisdiction of both law enforcement agencies (e.g., county sheriff) and correctional agencies (e.g., county probation departments, and state corrections). The underlying assumption of the process is that correctional "treatment" should be reserved for those persons who pose a genuine threat to others, and that it should not be applied to non-serious offenders.

Some of the duties that can be associated with corrections include:

- Providing presentence investigation reports and information as appropriate.
- Furnishing probation supervision.
- Providing or facilitating the availability of official counseling/treatment as appropriate.
- Maintaining custodial control of the offender and assuring his safety, welfare and the safety of society.
- Facilitating or furnishing custodial programs encouraging rehabilitation to include: vocational training, academic education, counseling, recreation and other special programs.

Briefly, the correctional subsystem seeks rehabilitation of the convicted offender.

Corrections, the least visible of the formal criminal justice system components, recently has been subjected to a new sense of urgency. This new pressure is guided by the principle that reformation, not incarceration or vindictive suffering, should be the purpose of penal treatment. These reform efforts have introduced the concepts of rehabilitation, diagnosis and classification, probation and parole into the correctional process.

The Executive Summary of a recent Commission (National Advisory Commission on Criminal Justice Standards and Goals, 1972, p. 43) summarizes this concept in the following comment:

> . . . figures on recidivism make it clear that society today is not protected—at least not for very long—by incarcerating offenders, for many offenders return to crime shortly after release

from prison. There is also evidence that many persons in prison do not need to be there to protect society. Many persons can serve their sentences in the community without undue danger to the public. There is substantial evidence that probation, fines, public service requirements, and restrictions are less costly than incarceration and consistently produce lower rates of recidivism. It is here that the challenge of the professional in corrections lies.

Related to the correctional phase of criminal justice, are community based programs. These include foster and group homes, guided group interaction programs, intensive community treatment programs, and halfway houses. Without a sense of "community," the crime prevention potential and sharing of mutual responsibility for the quality of criminal justice is unfulfilled. But much like the institutionalized elements of the system, community based agencies are burdened with their own problems. These problems usually center around the conflict of acceptance and the lack of bureaucratic structure typically associated with a formal element of the system. For example:

- Services available are unknown to either the offender or members of criminal justice agencies.
- Many of the community agencies are in competition by duplicating services while needed services go unmet.
- Because of the inherent nature of volunteer resources, the quality and reliability of services provided tend to be non-available or non-uniform.
- Criminal justice agencies are conservative in their willingness to employ community based programs because the responsibility for the offender always remains, by law, with the agencies and not with the community group.

A general failure to appreciate the intricacies, problems, and interrelationship of criminal justice agencies has been a primary factor in the lack of cooperation that exists between criminal justice agencies and community based programs.

Perhaps our criminal justice system would better be described as a process. This process then, involves the decisions and actions taken by an institution, offender, victim or society which influence the offender's movement into, through or out of the criminal justice system. Consequently this process also influences the system itself, either "horizontally", between one functional unit and another, or "vertically" within a single functional unit. Horizontal effects are a result of such factors as the amount of crime (which influences police and prosecutor activity and society frustration); the number of prosecutions (which influences court and defense attorney activities; and the type of court disposition affecting the population in correctional facilities and rehabilitative programs. Vertical effects are exemplified by court appeals (the number determining the workload of appellate courts) and by appellate court reversals of trial court decisions. This process can be illustrated by Figure I-2.

No one part of the criminal justice system can reduce crime by itself nor can it afford to be insensitive to the concerns and objectives of the other parts. In actuality, the criminal justice system is of limited significance in preventing crime. Police on every city block, three times the existing number of prosecutors and judges, and redoing our correctional attitudes and programs will have but a limited effect on the total crime rate. Rather, the principal role of the criminal justice system must be to ensure justice—including fair and objective assessment coupled with the protection of constitutional rights.

The prevention of crime must begin much earlier than one's first contact with the system. As indicated by a national study (President's Commission on Law Enforcement and Administration of Justice 1967, p. 17,):

> We will not have dealt effectively with crime until we have alleviated the conditions that stimulate it. To speak of controlling crime only in terms of the work of the police, the courts, and the correctional apparatus is to refuse to face the fact that widespread crime implies a widespread failure by society as a whole.

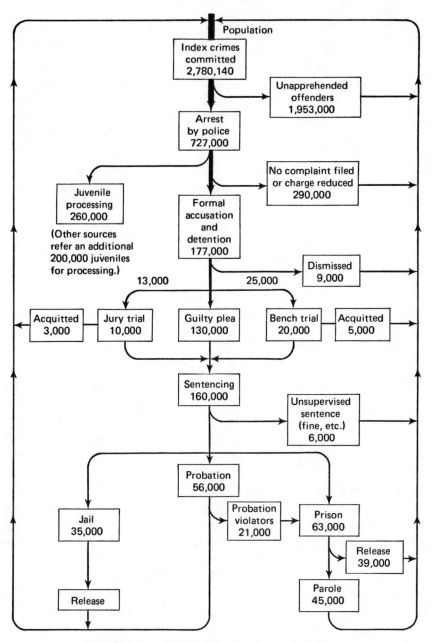

FIGURE I-2. Criminal Justice System Model.

Source: Adapted from the President's Commission on Law Enforcement and Administration of Justice, *The Challenge of Crime in a Free Society* (Washington, D.C.: Government Printing Office, 1967), pp. 262-263.

The Need for Criminal Justice Planning

The problems experienced by the elements of the criminal justice system have grown out of their organizational and administrative fragmentations. There is fragmentation among the components of the system, fragmentation within individual components, and fragmentation among political jurisdictions having various measures of authority over individual components. System-wide criminal justice planning including contributions by each agency of the system, provides a practical methodology to bring effective operation to the complex pursuit of criminal justice goals. Planning is the basic solution for any successful action seeking to integrate needs and to coordinate the fragmented segments of the criminal justice system within, between and among its various components and elements.

Describing Planning Benefits

The scope of criminal justice planning will often transcend jurisdictional and individual agency responsibilities. Goals derived from a successful planning program will help delineate the relationships among the criminal justice agencies and the related public and community programs. These goals can frequently be directed toward multiple agency or even regional programs in an effort to reduce duplication of effort and attack crime on a more comprehensive front.

All elements of the criminal justice system should be included in the planning process in order that the resulting goals will be realistically related to the needs of the society. This does not mean that individual agencies should not do their own planning. In fact, just the opposite is true. It means that agency plans must be coordinated to assure non-conflict in furthering the system towards its established goals. Generally, criminal justice planning will encourage each component to more effectively identify their own particular problem areas. Planning will provide a framework for determining priorities, encourage consideration of alternative courses of action, and assist in the anticipation of problems, thereby permitting the system component an opportunity to become goal and objective oriented rather than system maintenance oriented.

More specifically, planning for criminal justice activities facilitates the below listed items:

Improved Unity of Purpose Among the Criminal Justice Components and the Units that Comprise the Components

Current expressed objectives of criminal justice components (or units within the components) often conflict. Police often view their primary purpose as to get the criminal off the street, yet corrections officials may see their role as one of rehabilitation, in which locking up a criminal has little positive value for the individual. Similar examples can be cited between departments in a criminal justice agency. The administrative division in a police department is concerned with maintaining neat, accurate and readily accessible files necessitating use of the patrolman's time in preparation. The patrolman, on the other hand, feels "paperwork" is wasting his time compared to "crime fighting". Somewhere between the police and corrections are the courts, trying to ensure a fair law application to all who are measured against it. However, the courts have sometimes worked at cross purposes to both police and corrections when recognizing the rights of groups and individuals as opposed to society at large. This is illustrated by recent Supreme Court decisions concerning the rights of the accused. A cooperative, comprehensive effort by all criminal justice components and units will help to identify their common interests and establish the direction in which the administration should proceed.

Improve Coordination of Effort Between and Within Political Jurisdictions

Many local governments are approaching insolvency because they are besieged on one side for a reduction or leveling off of the tax rate, and on the other, by the citizen's desire for increased and improved services. Criminal justice planning, while not directly providing tax relief, can promote coordination among local jurisdictions, components within jurisdictions and, units within components leading to the more efficient allocation of resources (such as streamlining unnecessary duplication of services), thereby reducing public expenses. A direct product of planning is a budget and schedule by programs that can be evaluated by pre-established criteria for success or failure.

Increased Positive Community Involvement

In addition to educating the public, involvement of the citizenry at certain stages of the planning process serves to provide a more constructive community relationship with criminal justice agencies. Improved citizen cooperation for both preventing and controlling crime can be expected if citizens are involved in pointing out problems and issues, and in reviewing and suggesting solutions. Most regional planning efforts established by the Crime Control Act of 1968 have active citizen-at-large members participating on their regional planning boards. Also recent nation-wide Criminal Justice Standards and Goals efforts have encouraged citizen participation in the planning process. Additionally, citizen resources can be coordinated to implement community based programs to relieve some of the criminal justice agency work-load. Other benefits associated with planning to be realized particularly by the agencies employing the process include:

- Identification and analysis of problems at departmental and agency levels.
- Recognition of needs through assessment of existing resources.
- Providing a method to define goals that can alleviate problems.
- Establishing a framework to guide the assignment of priorities for allocating resources.
- Encouraging the consideration of various courses of action for reaching a goal and help in the selection of a preferred choice.
- Establishing formats for information reporting at each planning level.
- Displaying milestones of accomplishment by which to judge progress, and

- Furnishing information to those who are involved in the design making process.

From the foregoing it would appear that planning might be the panacea to all problems; however, such is not the case. Planning does provide a warning mechanism to facilitate early problem identification which, when isolated, can be solved.

The Planning Process

Planning should be dynamic in nature and should be regarded as a continuing process—constantly in progress rather than beginning each spring and ending the following winter —without a defined end.

Planning must be regarded as an inseparable part of the management process. It is essential to good, efficient administration. Major functions of planning are the identification of deficiencies, opportunities, and threats to the criminal justice system.

The result of this process is the documentation of a comprehensive plan to report each major step and provide a blueprint for action, as well as establishing the framework around which agencies and units of local government may concentrate their efforts.

Successful planning requires the active support and encouragement of policy makers. If planning is to play a vital role within an organization, policy makers must be committed to it and make this commitment known. Such a commitment implies the willingness to take actions and to improve one's environment, both internally and externally. Another ingredient of a successful planning process is that staff, responsible for planning, have the confidence of the major policy makers.

Planning requires a blend of planning-oriented and operational staff, properly selected, to bring a broad spectrum of expertise and knowledge to the system. Generally, such a group can be more constructive since individual nonobjectivity becomes more difficult and self-serving findings are less likely to result.

It must be remembered that there exists within most organizations a basic conflict between planning and day-to-day operations. One source of the irritation is planning's constant search for the identification and improvement of problem areas, which may be considered a reflection on the capabilities of operational management.

Planning needs to be conducted in the open and not in a vacuum. An aim of planners should be the constant education of themselves and others as to the purpose and content of planning efforts. It is particularly important to remember that key personnel must be kept informed and involved in the planning process. Further, planners cannot afford to be afraid of controversy because, by its very nature, a good planning process questions current activities, examines results, and creates controversy.

Maintaining objectivity is of primary importance—lack of which often is the single greatest cause of error in any planning process and must be overcome if planning is to be successful.

There is also the need for developing applicable fiscal and information data bases. Current types of criminal justice fiscal and information systems were developed without planning in mind and leave much to be desired. However, they do serve as a base from which meaningful data may be constructed. A mistake many planning bodies make is the collection of too much useless data. To avoid this, it is important to determine what data are required, whether the data are available, and the collection techniques to be used.

The planning process must be the result of an orderly development. By its very nature a planning process should be specific, well-conceived, and flexible. It is necessary to remember that while the planning process is essential, it is the results of the implemented improvements that are of primary interest.

Planning Steps

Within any planning process there exists a series of tasks necessary to its successful operation. The basic steps of the process set forth in this text are depicted in Figure I-3. Identify-

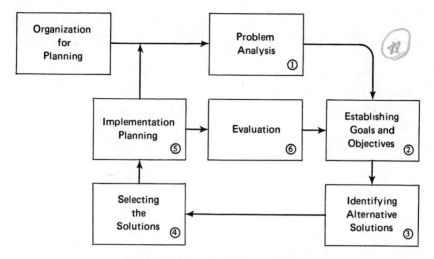

FIGURE I-3. The Planning Process.

ing problem areas is the first step. Other steps within this process are establishing goals and objectives, identifying alternative solutions, selecting the solutions and implementation of planning and evaluation. Each of the steps, from the first to the last, represents a distinct link in the process.

Planning in the criminal justice system should begin with a perspective of the total system (prevention, control, adjudication, and rehabilitation). The performance of the complete system is examined with the intention of flagging problem areas.

Problem analysis cannot be overlooked as it provides a focus for the planning process and is useful in maintaining coordination throughout the process.

The purpose of establishing goals and objectives is to set forth clearly the agreed aims of a particular group of criminal justice agencies, or of a single agency of the system.

Goal and objective setting is used to communicate the intent and direction that policy makers plan to take and the resources they may wish to commit.

Identifying alternative solutions begins with identifying the involvement of components and units of the criminal justice system in attaining the stated goals. From here, alternative plans are developed in detail, including schedules, constraints, resources required, impact, and organizational effects. During this step, criteria for selection among the alternatives are established.

The selection of the solutions may be done by a number of methods, including intuition and systems analysis, to name but two. In practice, selection is usually the result of considering numerous factors among which might be ability to meet stated goals effectively, probability of success, cost effectiveness, and compatibility with present resources.

The next step in the process is the implementation of the chosen solution. This includes the development of detailed work plans.

The last step in the planning process is to monitor and evaluate the planning effort. The evaluation step is the process that closes the loop and permits one to determine:

- if the activity is on schedule and within the pre-planned resource usage, and
- if it is accomplishing the goals and objectives it initially undertook.

The remainder of this book will cover in detail each of the steps in the planning process. It will relate these examples. It is the intent of this text to provide the practical planner with operational tools for accomplishing his task.

Planning vs. Plans

While the words are similar and interrelated, there is a fundamental difference between planning and plans. Planning is a basic organic function of management. It is a mental process of thinking through the desired and how it will be achieved. A plan is the tangible evidence of the thinking of the management. It results from planning. Plans are commitments to specific courses of action growing out of the mental process of planning. The planning process need not necessarily result in written plans; plans can be unwritten or expressed orally.

Types of Plans

By definition a plan is a documentation of a projected course of action; thus planning means determining what shall be done. There are many ways to classify plans. For example the dichotomy of single-use plans and standardized plans. Single-use plans lay out one course of action to fit a special situation and are used up when the objectives are satisfied. Once designated, standing plans are used continuously with periodic updates (sometimes called a Master Plan or comprehensive plan).

Another classification refers to relative time intervals anticipated by plans: short-range plans and long-range plans. Short-range plans tend to have relatively inflexible goals. These goals should be made compatible with and unified by long-range goals. Long-range plans, which have more flexible goals, are not so well defined in procedure. As we move up the hierarchical scale, the next classification of plans are strategic and tactical plans. Strategic planning is the process of determining the major goals and objectives of a criminal justice agency and the policies and strategies that will govern the acquisition, use, and disposition of resources to achieve those goals and objectives. The strategic planning process includes missions or purposes, if they have not been determined previously, and the specific objectives that are sought by an agency. Although the strategic plans are usually long-range, they can be short-range. In this area we are dealing with the major, the most important and basic objectives, policies and strategies of an element of the criminal justice system.

Tactical plans, on the other hand, relate to lower management levels. They are usually done on a periodic cycle that is on a fixed time schedule. Tactical planning is normally accomplished in greater detail and considers fewer alternative solutions. Uncertainty is less in tactical plans. Tactical planning problems are more structured and often repetitive in nature. They are usually the short-range type but can be long-range. Tactical plans should fall within parameters of strategic plans and usually entail greater details that are easy to evaluate.

A tactical plan for a police department might include a procedure for handling the looting of downtown merchants' shops during a general civil disorder. The strategic plan on the other hand would be comprised of many tactical plans and be a total coordinating procedure for the handling of civil disorders.

The last order of plans concerns the direction in which planning and solution implementation is to be expended. The first category is crime oriented planning, that approaches criminal justice problems by considering subproblems categorized by the type of offense. In order to effect a reduction of crime, the planning effort must be specifically directed toward that end. Crime specific planning is an attempt to develop strategies and tactics to overcome known crime problems and rapidly identify emerging crimes. The counterpart of crime oriented planning and the second category is system improvement planning and plans. These are plans that are created to produce improvement in the facilities, process or manpower of the criminal justice system, whose improvement may or may not directly relate to the crime reduction process. There comes a point, for example, where a new jail must be built, not because it may reduce crime, but because of safety and humane factors toward inmates and responsible guards. Other examples include communication and management information systems. The foregoing discussion of plans and their relationship to one another are summarized in Figure I-4.

The planning process and methodologies illustrated in the text are applicable to each of the foregoing types of plans described. The remainder of this text focuses on the planning process. The reader should determine the type of plan that meets his agency's need and initiate the appropriate planning process.

Summary

The criminal justice system defies a clear-cut definition, complicated by the roles and responsibilities of its several elements. We soon realize that the system is a non-system that functions as a process. Planning then provides a primary method by which this process can be harmonized to insure that common or non-conflicting objectives are being attained by each of the systems elements, components and units. Further we learn

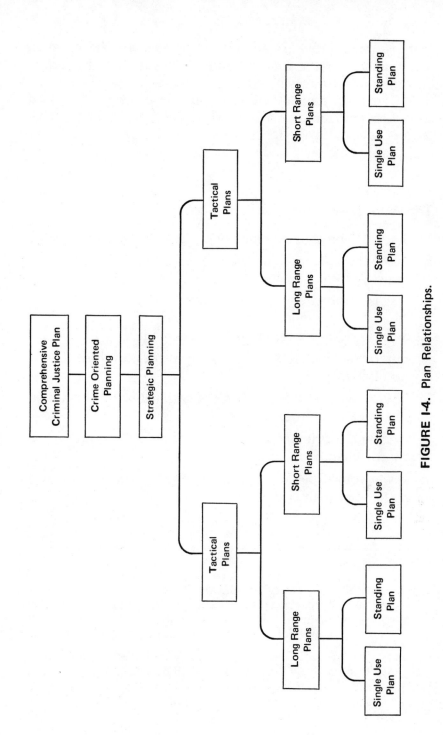

FIGURE 1-4. Plan Relationships.

that planning provides an invaluable tool for the criminal justice administrator, assisting him in the timely and effective allocation of resources based upon the logic of need.

The basic steps of the planning process were discussed and a differentiation is made between plans and planning. This chapter sets the stage for the remaining chapters in this text and should be clearly understood.

Topics for Discussion

1. Discuss the role of the criminal justice system in our society.
2. Name the influences that impact a county level criminal justice system.
3. Discuss the consequences of justice system conflict between the major components—law enforcements, courts, corrections and community based activities.
4. Differentiate between the planning process and the scientific process.
5. Discuss what is meant when the criminal justice system is described as a process.
6. Discuss the difference between crime reduction and system improvement planning.
7. Relate your experiences with a planning process used in areas other than criminal justice.

REFERENCES

Ackoff, Russel L., *A Concept of Corporate Planning*, New York: Wiley and Sons, 1970. Presents a systematic and practical treatment of corporate planning. The text concentrates on the nature of planning, methodology, techniques and philosophy.

Cleland, David I., and William R. King, *Systems Analysis and Project Management*, New York: McGraw-Hill Book Co., 1968. This text applies the systems approach in looking at managerial functions. Selected chapters discuss project management, planning and control.

Drucker, Peter F., *Management-Tasks, Responsibilities and Practices*, New York: Harper and Row, Publishers, 1974. This text focuses on management and the tasks a manager performs. It takes an in-depth look into the managerial tasks of planning and control as well as other selected tasks.

Eastman, George, ed., *Municipal Police Administration*, Washington, D.C.: International City Management Association, 1969. Provides an overview of police administration duties and responsibilities. Material covers police organization principles, planning and functional descriptions of investigation and patrol.

National Advisory Commission on Criminal Justice Standards and Goals, *Executive Summary*, Washington, D.C.: U. S. Government Printing Office, 1974, p. 81. This executive summary reflects the major proposals in the six reports of the National Advisory Commission on Criminal Justice Standards and Goals.

President's Commission on Law Enforcement and the Administration of Justice, *The Challenge of Crime in a Free Society*, Washington, D.C.: U. S. Government Printing Office, 1967. The founding document that resulted in the Omnibus Crime Control and Safe Streets Act of 1968 and the Law Enforcement Assistance Administration.

Chapter Objectives

1. Defines the importance of need determination.
2. Establishes idea sources, differentiating between internal and external influences.
3. Shows the relationship among idea sources, need determination and plan development.
4. Introduces the process of problem identification.
5. Recognizes constraints on solution of major problems.
6. Determines problem parameters.
7. Introduces the reader to the concept of establishing goals and objectives.
8. Provides the reader with an understanding of the goals and objectives setting process.

2

Problem Analysis—
Establishing Goals
And Objectives

The initial chapter has introduced the reader to the criminal justice planning process and to the different types of planning. Now it is necessary to learn how to identify the key problem(s) and to develop techniques whereby the problem(s) may be resolved.

The purpose of this chapter is threefold. First, the reader is introduced to a problem analysis approach. The specific objectives are to:

- introduce the philosophy of analyzing problems.
- develop an awareness of problem identification.
- provide a simplified approach to the subject of problem analysis.

Secondly, this chapter has been purposely designed to acquaint the reader with the perspectives of goal and objective setting in the Criminal Justice System. It provides some examples and the relationship of:

- goals to objectives
- priority of goals and objectives to planning.

Thirdly, the chapter attempts to show the reader, by combining these two subjects into a single chapter, the need to realize and understand planning dynamics.

Need Determination

Of primary importance to the development of a plan is the realization that a need exists, or that there is at least adequate concern for the preparation of a feasibility study. Recognition of a need is the first step in the planning process. It is an important step, for if real needs are not being responded to, an organization (or in this case a criminal justice agency) will not be performing at maximum ability or efficiency.

Since criminal justice agencies are non-profit organizations in the same sense as a company or corporation, the realization of maximum performance may be somewhat elusive. Where a company has the definite incentive of profit or loss, the criminal justice agency deals with people. The agency therefore must be cognizant of and responsible to community problems and needs.

Idea sources for a planner's optional choice fall into two categories labeled internal and external.

Internal and External Influences

The most obvious idea source, identified as an internal influence, is the chief executive. Often the planner is not the chief or senior executive. In which case, utilization of his knowledge as a potential source of ideas, is a good idea in itself. A chief executive has spent a considerable amount of time observing the agency's performance from every aspect. He has thought through possible problem areas and improvement needs. He is also the best source for obtaining a complete understanding of the criminal justice system's (as well as his own agency's) goals and objectives. Consequently when confronted with a need or problem, he will be able to mentally place it in priority and provide the planner with considerable insight.

Other senior management levels are also potentially excellent sources of ideas. They, relative to their own respective roles, can give the planner much information about a unit's problems, function, capability and limitations. Collectively or singularly, depending on the planner's need, management can be an extremely important idea source.

Another internal source is the agency personnel. They deal with the day to day routine of agency operation, and often can see a problem arising or existing, but unnoticed by higher levels of management. Several ways of acquiring these ideas are not uncommon. Employee suggestion boxes is a possibility. This method has been utilized by the private business sector, and has met with some degree of success. In most cases, however, use of this method presupposes an attached incentive varying from money, promotion, and esteem, to a combination of these. Another possibility would be for the planner to spend time talking with agency personnel individually. Good rapport can lead to voluntary suggestions or comments that collectively could be helpful in resolving a particular problem. In either case, continued openness by agency personnel will depend upon the planner's ability and sincerity in affecting changes where needed.

The planner can, through the chief executive, establish a built in signal device to indicate certain problem areas without relying solely on total personnel participation and Labreton and Henning (1961) call this "formal control." They state:

> The basic requirement for successful control consists of a set of standards for each significant item which reflects anticipated and desired performance and on an acceptable range of variation from ideal performance.

Relating this to the criminal justice system, the method utilized in an agency's reporting procedure could conform to the formal control concept in helping to determine a problem area or need. In this case, submitting a report causes an automatic, or nearly automatic response to take place. Supervisors monitoring their areas of responsibility can discern a problem and report it to the planner.

Meetings among agency executives and planners can be useful in the determination of problem areas, and can be a valuable idea source. This method works if the key players will participate and discuss their needs and desires openly. This type of planning discussion can be helpful in warding off interagency problems within the criminal justice system. The following example is indicative of what can happen where interagency planning is lacking. A lower court establishes a diagnostic project which will provide medical, psychological, economic, and educational information about a subject prior to sentencing. The court does not have the administrative capability to handle the project, so the court asks the probation department to manage the project. After a time, however, the chief probation officer comes to realize this additional workload is requiring numerous staff hours to satisfy the demands of the project. Then as budget hearings commence, the local governing officials get upset when the chief probation officer adds a new position to his next year's budget. The impact of such situations causes many people to be upset. Such situations need not occur with proper planning.

The most significant outside source to the local criminal justice system is the community. The community will react to their areas of concern. Since the community is generally so diverse, areas of concern pointed out by different groups or individuals will usually be issue oriented and aimed at particular departmental levels, i.e., policy/management, supervisorial, or functional. The planner can utilize community input as issues and problems arise within the system or a particular agency. Input of this type can be valuable in developing questionnaires used in attitude surveys which address the nature of the issue or problem.

Causative Relationship

Good agency planning is continuous. The planner, be he chief executive or department head, should continue to feel the pressures of planning requirements. In a theoretical sense, no plan should appear in final form. Draft plans maintain the aura of flexibility, change, and improvement. The planning process does not even begin with a problem. Rather there is an inescapable relationship among causative factors, problem and need determination, and plan development. Simply expressed, the relationship can be visualized as follows in Figure II-1. The agency planners must recognize this relationship, to insure the

Causative Factors	Prob/Need Determinator	Plan Development
internal influences	realization/analysis of causes	objectives
external influences		

FIGURE II-1. Causitive Relationship.

direction that agency planning takes is toward the solution of real problems.

Problem Identification

Problem identification includes:
- Establishing the boundaries of the problem, and
- Quantitatively and qualitatively describing the problem.

The general boundaries of a problem can be circumscribed by stating some demographic constraints identifying the parameters of the problem. For example, we are only concerned with the problems that are indigenous to police department X, county Y, or a given state.

A second general boundary consideration is to limit the problem development process to those areas where criminal justice planning professionals feel the problems may exist. Thus, the professional is given credit for knowing his business. Examples might include focusing attention on problem development related to:

- Crime, for a police department,
- Case load management, for a probation department, or
- Trial delay, for a court.

Data Gathering and Analysis

The next step in the identification process is to develop the problem quantitatively as well as qualitatively. This involves researching and analyzing the problem area from viewpoints of:

- Statistics, or statistical analysis
- The people working in the department area, or Delphi Analysis, and
- Lastly, the customer viewpoint, or attitude survey.

As shown in Figure II-2 we are seeking those problems which are similarly identified by all three viewpoints; those

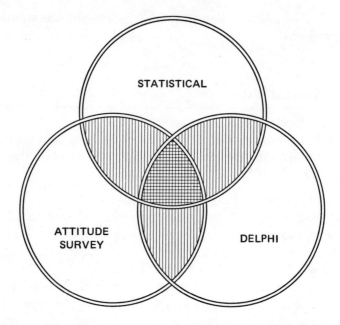

FIGURE II-2. View of Problem List Criteria.

identified by only two viewpoints; and those supported by only one viewpoint. These form our problem area list.

Hoffman points out that (Hoffman, 1972):

Few areas rely more heavily on statistics than the criminal justice system and, specifically, the law enforcement profession. Crime statistics reported in the Uniform Crime Report, published annually by the FBI, is the basis for determining the level of the nation's criminal activity. Trends in the types of crimes being committed, by whom, when, and where are meaningful, within limits, in the detection of criminal patterns and the prediction of certain types of criminal behavior. But, the interpretation of crime statistics must be handled carefully.

Crime statistics are only as useful as they are accurate, and a significant percentage of reported crimes are inaccurately reported. In addition, it has been estimated that only one-quarter to one-half of all crimes committed ever get reported. The incidence of unreported crime is highest in the inner-city areas where crime is the highest and where confidence in and respect for law enforcement is the lowest. Yet, this is precisely where the focus on the nature of crime and criminal behavior should be closest. Crime statistics must be reported in rates per population and must be related to population growth, income levels, education, and welfare rolls.

Because crime rates play an important role in society's fear of crime, and because an intelligent approach to crime statistics, to rates of recidivism, to case loads, and the like can yield worthwhile information, such information should be an integral part of problem identification.

A more detailed discussion on data gathering, analysis and technique is contained in subsequent chapters.

Define General Problem Areas

A problem is an existing difficult and unsettled situation requiring a solution that will improve the situation and make it more acceptable. The following is an example of a problem:

The use of dangerous drugs and narcotics has increased to severe proportions in a specific community.

The objective of this task is the identification of a complete list of general problem areas. This list provides the basis for selecting and documenting the major problems facing the planner and his agency or department.

Survey Existing Reports and Concerned Groups

A key starting point in developing this list is the review of existing written descriptions of problems in the criminal justice system. Existing routine reports, of course, provide indications or problem areas. Other common sources include the following:

- Reports by other agencies within the criminal justice system including previous planning efforts by local criminal justice planning agencies.
- Reports from local citizen's groups or those published in local newspapers.

- Problems, goals, and priorities identified in state or national plans.
- Recent articles, books, and other publications.
- Statistical information provided by the State Department of Justice, Bureau of Criminal Statistics.

A second key starting point in developing this list is the collective judgment, or opinion, of individuals or groups concerned with the criminal justice system including:

- Elected representatives.
- Top administrators.
- Staff and line personnel.
- Community organizations.
- General public.

List General Problem Areas

A list of general problem areas should be developed, and grouped into categories such as:

- Rapid change in expectations of criminal justice.
- Ineffective prevention and deterrence.
- Rising crime rate.
- System overhead due to traffic violations, intoxication, and other minor offenses.
- Fragmentation and duplication of criminal justice activities.
- Antiquated management practices.
- Inadequate and obsolete facilities.
- Statutes that hinder improvement.

Document the Major Problems Facing The Criminal Justice Agency

The objective of this task is to select and further define the major problems facing the criminal justice agency. An initial starting point might be the tentative listing discussed above, or the judgment of supervisors/department heads and staff. As the planning process is improved, problem areas may be tentatively defined by predictive models of the criminal justice system. The following tasks are generally required.

Establish Criteria for Acceptable Problem Statements

The requirements for an acceptable problem statement should be clearly articulated. For example, an acceptable problem statement:

- Contains a narrative description (i.e., a statement, as precise as possible, which describes the nature and seriousness of the problem).
- Contains a quantitative description (i.e., an estimate of the magnitude or extent of the problem in numerical terms, based on available statistics or informed judgment).
- Is expressed from one of the following perspectives:
  - types of crimes (e.g., narcotics, burglaries),
  - criminal justice systems (i.e., the capability of the system to provide the type and quality of services required.
  - offender profiles
  - victim response
  - community environment and resources (i.e., the contribution of conditions in the community to crime and to diversion of offenders; the effect of crime on life in the community).
  - target areas
  - transportation pattern
  - modus operandi
- Is qualified by such information as:
  - data sources used (e.g., statistical summaries, surveys, expert opinions),
  - geographical areas and population groups affected
  - criminal justice components involved

Select and Analyze Specific Problem Areas

Policy makers of the planning organization must be involved in the selection of the problem areas that will be subject to further definition and analysis. The actual selection and analysis might be performed by one of the following groups:

- By the planning staff, for review and action by policy makers. This approach is preferred where the planning staff is adequate in size and experience and where it has the confidence and respect of the policy makers.
- By a committee consisting of top administrators. These individuals usually offer the most experience and knowledge. As a group they can be more objective because there is less individual fear of the critical conclusion, and the self-serving finding is less likely to emerge. As this group will be involved in directing the implementation of improvements, they should be involved throughout the planning process.
- By a committee consisting of junior administrators for review and action by policy makers. This group is generally closer to operating detail and tends to retain more idealism and to be less compromising in judgments.
- By outside consultants, for review and action by policy makers. Outside consultants can provide a valuable service in this diagnostic phase of planning, particularly if internal conditions are not suitable for an in-house effort.

Building on the techniques of data analysis discussed in Chapter III, additional data must be gathered to measure and test hypotheses related to the selected problem areas. The choice of data collection techniques is determined by the following considerations:

- The amount of pertinent data needed to statistically define the problem.
- The resources available to collect data (personnel, time, files).
- The accessibility of the data (whether the data exist in the proper format, at a convenient location).

As data are collected, there should be a continual review in the following terms:

- Completeness—does the data cover all aspects of the problems?
- Adequacy—are there enough data to make definitive statements about the problem?
- Accuracy—have the data been recorded correctly?

It should not be expected that all data collected would meet such criteria, but any major inadequacies should be described and available to the decision-maker.

Major Problems Facing the Criminal Justice Agency

The outputs of this task should be the documentation of major problems. The documentation of these problem statements serves two primary purposes:

- Establishment of a focus for planning activities.
- Means of communicating among planners, officials, and the public.

The use of dangerous drugs and narcotics has increased to severe proportions in our community

- There are limited educational programs for youth and adults on the hazards of narcotics and dangerous drugs

- The drug arrest rate for juveniles has increased 65% in three years from 20 per 1000 to 33 per 1000

- The drug arrest rate for adults has increased 37% in three years from 30 per 1000 to 41 per 1000

- Narcotics and drug abuse cases now comprise 36% of the court calendar or 604 of 1680 cases

- Treatment programs for narcotics and dangerous drug users have been notably unsuccessful with a 25% revocation rate

- Treatment programs provided by resources outside of the criminal justice system are inadequate

---

FIGURE II-3. Example Problem Statement.

Recognize Constraints on Solving Major Problems

The final effort in this task is the acknowledgment of constraints, or external forces over which the planner or his organization has little or no control, which will limit the success of dealing with the major problems. Examples of these constraints, that will determine the feasibility of an alternative improvement, are:

- Technical—What new equipment, special skills, or new operations are required?
- Organizational—What is the organizational impact on the agencies affected in implementation? What is their reaction?
- Social—What is the expected public reaction and participation?
- Related programs—What are the difficulties in coordinating with other related programs?
- Economic—How much of the available resources will be consumed?
- Legal—What legislation is required?
- Political—What political factors will impact upon implementation?
- Demographic—Will implementation have a general effect or be more selective?
- Geographic—What is the expected scope of impact in relation to the above?

It is important as a planner to be aware of the constraints a plan is likely to engender. Not that the planner must yield to the pressures of a few, but neither should the process be a sole source endeavor.

Problem Parameters

When a planner begins to utilize any type of statistical analysis he must be mindful of the degree of involvement contemplated and the level of sophistication required to obtain needed information. In other words, jurisdictions and criminal justice agencies come in all sizes, and statistical analysis can vary from a simple percent to factor analysis and multiple regression techniques. Generally more worthwhile information is obtained the further you go; however, the degree of difficulty increases also. The planner's own capability must be considered where sophisticated techniques are to be utilized. Possibilities for the need of outside resources, i.e., consultant services, should be evaluated.

There are some simple, generally acceptable statistical analysis approaches to problem identification. These take the form of the traditional approach to the planner's needs.

Five basic problem parameters are easily obtained and will provide the planner with an understanding of important problem areas. These are as follows:

- Magnitude
- Rate of change
- Seriousness
- Location
- Who

What is being asked is:

- What is the extent of the problem?
- How is the problem changing (increasing or decreasing) and how fast?
- How many people does the problem affect, and how does the problem compare with similar problems in other locations?
- Where does the problem occur: what beat, city, county or agency is the greatest contributor to the problem; where is it growing at the fastest rate; where is it most serious?
- Who is causing the problem—generally speaking?

Magnitude

The magnitude of a problem can be determined by computing the percentage it represents in terms of the whole. For example, if out of 15,000 crimes reported there were 4000 burglaries, then burglaries represent 27% of the total. (4000 / 15000 × 100 = 27%). Magnitude gives the planner a rough picture as to the extent of the problems in relation to other crime problem areas. extent of the problems in relation to other crime problem areas.

Rate of Change

This parameter indicates how the problem is changing over a period of time. Small variations showing increases or decreases are expected on a yearly basis. What the planner is looking for here are some significant changes. Using the same example, say there were 4500 burglaries the year before, then the difference divided by the previous year figure (in this case 4500) gives a rate of change for that period. 4000 burglaries (current year) minus 4500 burglaries (previous year) = − 500 burglaries difference + or −. − 500 (difference) / 4500 (previous year) × 100 = − 11% rate of change. In this case, a decrease of 11% over the previous year.

Relative Seriousness

This parameter tells the planner on a comparative basis, the extent to which one community faces a problem relative to another. The community may be another jurisdiction of similar size, or a much larger one as a county or state. It can also give a rough idea of how many people are affected. For this calculation, population totals are needed. For example, if those same 4000 burglaries occurred within a community of 250,000 people then 1600 out of every 100,000 people, or about 1 out of every 63 people are being burglarized. (Remember you are interested in the rate per 100,000 people). Then 250,000 equals 2.5 times 100,000, therefore 4000 (burglaries) / 2.5 (100,000 people) = 1600 burglaries per 100,000 people. If you wish to know roughly how many people are affected out of each 100,000, divide 100,000 by 1600 and you obtain 1 out of every 63.

You may take this further if you like. Assume an average of 4 people per family, then 1 out of every 16 families are personally affected (63 ÷ 4 = 16 approximately). Similar calculations with data obtained from another jurisdiction will provide a comparison. Some planners prefer to use a rate per 1000 in which case in the initial calculation you would divide by 250 instead of 2.5 (250 times 100 = 250,000). You would still determine 1 out of every 63 people are affected, and similarly 1 out of every 16 families.

By comparing figures with some other jurisdiction (i.e. city, county, state) you can determine if your jurisdiction is significantly higher or lower, thereby giving you a seriousness factor relative to that experienced in other areas.

Location

Location simply means where the problem is occurring. The planner should know the general boundaries with which he is dealing. It could be, for example, that the problem is so general that all the planner can say is that it's county wide. Perhaps, though, one city out of five in the county has the problem to a greater degree. Determining the problem by degree or determining who's got it the worst, does not lessen the problem in the other areas. It just gives the planner one more piece of information in terms of problem identification.

Who

Generally speaking, who is committing the crime? Arrest reports will give some explanation. From a statistical point of view one must ask; is the problem caused by adult, juvenile, male or female offenders? Further information can be obtained describing social, educational, and economic background. In addition to statistical analysis, two other techniques can be used to corroborate findings. One is the Delphi analysis, the other is Attitude survey.

Delphi Analysis

Planning must take into account both the actual and perceived. That is, what is true and what people believe to be true. In addition to the analysis of data which essentially reflects what is actually occuring, there is a definite need to question those who are actually involved with the criminal justice system (i.e., police, lawyers, judges, probation, corrections, criminals). The attitudes and relationship among the disassociated segments of the system and the elected officials with whom they relate are critical to the performance of planning objectives and pro- grams, and any long-term reform. The key to success of any plan is the total involvement of these individuals from problem identification to assessment of priorities. One thing to re- member is, if key personnel are not in the plan's development, they can be expected to be equally aloof regarding its implementation.

The essence of the Delphi technique is the ability to first solicit unheard individual opinions on a given issue and then share these personal responses with the total group. This allows additional input and individual reevaluation. As the process continues one or more ideas emerge that address the problem.

The Attitude Survey

Equally important for meaningful input into the problem identification process is from the community at large. While it is true that most members of society lack an acute understand- ing of the details of the criminal justice system, they do know what bothers them. The community can also provide informa- tion relating to what they would like to see more of and conversely, what less. Their perceptions of problems, whether general or more specific, relating to crime need to be compared with those ideas perceived through the Delphi analysis. In addition, community perception of crime problems can be compared with the problems identified through statistical analysis.

Finally, the planner can determine the relationship the various problem areas have with one another. This is a useful tool when establishing goals, objectives, and priorities in the planning process. To accomplish this, a matrix can be prepared utilizing the information obtained for each problem area based upon the problem parameters, Delphi analysis and Attitude survey. Of the five parameters, magnitude, rate of change, and seriousness become a part of the matrix. The problem areas are ranked in order of priority, number 1 being the highest priority, based on the criteria for each parameter. Similarly, problem areas are ranked according to the results of both the Delphi analysis, and Attitude survey. The summation of the matrix gives the planner an idea of his most pressing problem, plus the relative relationship of other problem areas. Figure II-4 gives an example of a matrix used in this fashion. In the example, Problem A, of the problems studied would receive first priority, because the matrix total for Problem A is the least. The second priority would be assigned to Problem C, followed by Problems B and D.

Establishing Goals and Objectives

Once a problem has been identified, and the decision has been made to resolve it, it is important to next develop it in perspective. In terms of a system problem for example, are you going to try to solve the whole thing or a part of it? Are you going to try to reduce crime or keep it from increasing too fast? Are you going to just look at specific crime areas? If so the same questions can be asked. And, of course, how are you going to

PROBLEM CRITERIA	PROBLEM A	PROBLEM B	PROBLEM C	PROBLEM D
MAGNITUDE	1	3	2	4
SERIOUSNESS	3	1	4	2
RATE OF CHANGE	2	4	3	1
DELPHI SURVEY	1	3	2	4
ATTITUDE SURVEY	4	2	1	3
TOTALS EACH ROW	11	13	12	14

FIGURE II-4. Problem Priority Matrix.

go about it? Establishing goals and objectives is the next paramount step toward any problem solution.

It is our objective to critically analyze and develop a sense of importance on how goals and objectives contribute to the planning process. The agencies making up the criminal justice system have traditionally lacked the understanding of formulating goals, to provide a framework for that agency to assess its effectiveness. Hopefully this chapter will provide insight into the process and the effect it has on the system of criminal justice.

Goals

Etzioni states that (Etzioni, 1964): "the goals of organizations serve many functions. They provide orientation by depicting a future state of affairs which the organization strives to realize. He further clarifies goals by stating the following:

> Goals constitute a source of legitimacy which justify the activities of the organization.
> Goals serve as standards by which members of an organization and outsiders assess the success of the organization (effectiveness and efficiency).

The importance of goal formulation as an integral part of the planning process is vital. The goal articulation defines the desired state of affairs that one is striving to achieve. Without the articulation of goals, planning becomes futile. One is left without the mission direction needed to develop and measure plans. This problem has plagued the criminal justice system and agencies within it. An attempt will now be made to build a framework of goal development for criminal justice agencies; a process which is drastically lacking in contemporary planning.

Goal Setting Process

In the context of the criminal justice system we view goals as a desired state of affairs for the system. One recent article indicates that (Leach, 1974): "the overall goal and purpose of the criminal justice system is the elimination of crime and delinquency". The author further qualifies this by contending that this statement of purpose seems obvious; however, many persons within the system do not function in relation to it.

Some judges just try cases. Some district attorneys just prosecute. Some police just catch offenders. Officials who so limit their roles indicate that they do not function in relation to the purpose of the system. Their goal is some subordinate part of the production line. They revere a bush or a rock rather than the universe (Leach, 1974, p. 37). Perhaps this view leads us to take a systematic look at the criminal justice system realizing that system components (police, courts, etc.) have an impact upon each other. If this is the case, the need to articulate criminal justice goals would seem obvious. The political subdivision of counties would appear the logical starting point for goal articulation, since each county has a representative criminal justice system. That is, all the components are operating at the county level. The goal setting could be done by a working board made up of representative heads of the agencies. To be effective, such goal setting would require executive level participation. The results might read as follows in a particular county:

1. Eliminate inappropriate use of criminal sanctions.
   a. develop new remedies for victimless crimes.
2. Reduce the processing time of offenders in the system.
   a. develop alternatives to arrest.
   b. develop common sense *speedy* trial and appeal procedures.

The point is, in order to adequately begin a system of planning one must begin to look at system goals as differentiated from isolated agency goals.

Objectives

Objectives are different from goals. They are more specific and are measurable against a dimension of time. For example, the goal to reduce processing time of offenders would have to be qualified with objectives. An illustration might read as follows:

- To reduce the criminal justice processing time of offenders by ten days within the next fiscal year.

This objective is measurable and has a specific time frame for accomplishment. The objectives provide a basis for looking at and brainstorming solutions or programs to meet the specific objective and thus achieving the goal.

The writing of objectives should meet the following criteria (City of Palo Alto, 1973):

- An objective must be stated in terms of results, not process or activities.
- The results of an objective must be specific not general and must be recognizable and understandable, so it will be recognized when objectives have been met.
- An objective must be measurable. The evaluation criteria should be built into the objective statement. This implies that the objective will be quantifiable.
- An objective must be achievable and feasible within specific time frames.
- An objective should be oriented to some audience or user of service.

Objectives that can meet the above criteria will provide a viable base for program procedures that will measure the program of an agency or division toward satisfying its objectives (City of Palo Alto, 1973).

There should be a definite link between the broad goal and specific objectives, as this serves as a foundation for evaluation. The need to establish the goal/objective relationship is vital. In the resource example at the end of the chapter is a determination of how problem determination, goal setting, and evaluation relate to each other as integral parts of the planning process.

The emphasis for criminal justice agencies to assess productivity and to be accountable for performance will present ever increasing challenges. The beginning of this is to develop a planning capability that can serve as the vehicle to assess productivity toward stated goals and objectives.

Summary

This chapter has attempted to point out a process through which a planner should approach problem analysis. It focuses on need determination, problem analysis, and the establishing of goals and objectives. Points to be considered are:

1. Need determination and the techniques associated with it.
2. Causative relationship.
3. Problem identification, and an idea of some methods which can be used relatively easily. More specifically, it says that problems are not just there, but there has to be a cause, and that these factors have a relationship that lasts through plan implementation. Also, problem identification and priority ranking could more candidly and accurately be expressed through a form of anonymity while maintaining the group process. And, finally, it provides an approach which is both philosophically and practically sound and may well reduce the planner's tendency to rely solely on professionals.

In addition, the chapter points out the very real need to establish goals and objectives in order to make planning meaningful.

Topics for Discussion

1. Why is it important to first determine a need?
2. Why is it important for the planner to develop good idea sources?
3. What is the significance behind an understanding of causative relationship?
4. What is the process involved with problem identification?

5. Why is it important to recognize constraints, particularly when seeking solutions to major problems?

6. How can the problem parameters mentioned in Chapter II be helpful to the criminal justice planner?

7. What is the difference between a goal and an objective?

8. Why is it important to follow the goal and objective setting process?

RESOURCE

A MODEL THIRD PARTY CUSTODY PROJECT*

Situation

The majority of offenders committing Impact target crimes appear to be from the same or very similar communities. Better than 75 percent of the perpetrators are black and from the lowest socioeconomic levels in the community. Furthermore, the ages of offenders appear to cluster in such a way that individuals drawn at random for a controlled experiment would be representative of the population from which they are selected. An experiment, then, could be conducted to determine the effectiveness of intensive counseling and referral services.

Planning

Purpose—To achieve a reduction in the arrest rate for Impact target crimes by providing supervisory custody and follow-up services to a selected group of offenders from the total program population. The aim is to divert offenders from the traditional criminal justice system by providing viable and responsive social service alternatives that realistically treat the needs of the target group.

Budget/Scope—$200,000 for each fiscal year, 1973 and 1974.

Agencies—Community Social Services Agency

---

*Source: Mitre Corporation, *Evaluation in Criminal Justice Programs: Guidelines and Examples*, LEAA, NILECJ, May, 1972.

Objective—To provide 600 juvenile and young adult Impact offenders third party supervisory custody and divert 300 of them from the criminal justice system. To determine techniques for measuring the effectiveness of such services in deterring the offender from future criminal activity (and also the value of such deterrence to society). To assess the impact of project services on two groups of project participants.

Implementation—An 11-man project staff, along with a 5-man Halfway House staff, will be organized to process offenders diverted from the Juvenile Court or by County Court by an intake counselor who screens them for their suitability for alternative treatment. Participants then are assigned to one of two experimental groups at random. Group I participants receive a battery of specialized services (residential care, counseling, short-term financial assistance, referral, etc.), while Group II receives monthly telephone contacts and initial urinalysis for potential assignment to a drug treatment program. The arrest records of both groups will be monitored to determine the degree to which Group I treatment is effective.

Constraints—None given.

Results Anticipated—A 50 percent reduction in the number of Impact target crimes committed by the sample population over the lifespan of the project.

Project Effectiveness

The effectiveness measures to determine project success are listed below:

1. Total number of offenders assigned to Experimental Group I who are arrested.
2. Total number of offenders assigned to Experimental Group II who are arrested.

As a means of providing data that will be useful in project evaluation, and in order that the juvenile court and prosecutor's office may have available current statistical information related to the project, a simplified information system will be devised. Report forms utilized will contain quantitative and narrative data on the operation of the project, and summary data on the population served.

Narrative data will include information such as project impact on offenders in the areas of employment stability and recidivism. Summary data will include information on individual offenders relative to specific problem areas.

Project Efficiency

The efficiency measures are:

1. Total number of offenders diverted to the Third Party Custody Project.
2. Biweekly qualitative summary data for both experimental groups.
3. Total number of dismissals of pending charges based on satisfactory project participation.
4. Total number of extensions of the court continuance date to allow more time for additional work with the offenders.
5. Total number of reversions (based on surrender of custody requests) to normal court processing.

Rearrest, alone, will not constitute grounds for returning an offender to the normal court routine. Such factors as offender attitude prior to rearrest, nature and type of offense in the new arrest, and narcotics use will be considered. Using a point system, a supervising counselor will determine when a written surrender of custody request is appropriate. This set of variables will apply equally to members of both groups.

6. Total number of Experimental Group I members that are gainfully employed.
7. Total number of Experimental Group II members that are gainfully employed.

A comparison will be made between employment levels for the two groups. Since the project will employ its own job development specialist, it is assumed that this professional will utilize every resource at his disposal to locate suitable employment opportunities for project offenders. The job development specialist will contact prospective employers by telephone to arrange interviews for the offenders who will be given a Third

Party Custody Project Care form to be filled out and returned by the prospective employer after the interview. Bus tokens and some short-term financial assistance will also be made available to members of Experimental Group I. Once an offender has become gainfully employed, monthly records of his wages will be tabulated by the assigned project counselor. This procedure will be followed for members of both groups.

Other evaluation measures, necessary to perform a complete evaluation of the level of project success, include the following:

a. If a drug abuser, the number of "dirty" urines during time in project.
b. If assisted find gainful employment, length of time on the job.
c. If placed in one-to-one counselling, attitudinal changes and how effected.
d. If placed in group counselling, number of times absent from the group. (In addition, relative position in group sociogram [see Section III for explanation].)
e. Number of voluntary drop-outs from project.

In the juvenile court, it is always necessary to identify an offender by such additional data as birthdate and/or names of parents or guardians. Problems in all of these areas will be greatly alleviated by providing all agencies that are to be contacted regularly with a list of names of project staff members eligible to receive such data.

The project will employ its own narcotics clerk who will collect the urine specimens required, as well as all other data relative to drug use and abuse. At least one specimen will be collected from every member of the project population at the time of admission to the project. All offenders whose urinalysis results are positive for drug use will be referred to an appropriate drug treatment program. Such referrals will exclude any youthful offender positive for methadone and involved in an approved methadone maintenance program.

Project counselors will collect all other pertinent data from their individual clients. Any problems in this area will likely be with verifications of offender statements. Some police jurisdictions, employers, and hospitals, for example, will only provide information upon written request accompanied by a release of confidential information form signed by the offender.

Data Collection

Project counselling staff will be responsible for the initial collection and progressive updating of all data on project offenders. Two members of the counselling team will be assigned to regular court duty on a weekly, rotating basis. The on-duty counselors will collect data on all offenders diverted to the project initially during their on-duty week. They will also share responsibility for getting diverted offenders from the court setting to the project office. If the offender requires 24-hour residential custody, initial processing is also the responsibility of the on-duty counselors.

All arrest record data will be collected from the police, FBI, courts, and probation and parole offices. Copies of the biweekly status reports on project offenders will be transmitted to the juvenile court, prosecutor's office, project director, and supervisor, with a single copy being retained in each offender's social file.

Data Management

Each offender in the target populace will have a social file containing copies of all data pertinent to his progress. A master card index will also be maintained with all pertinent identifying data for each project offender. These will be color-coded to differentiate between Experiment Group I and Experimental Group II members. All required data will be collected and funneled to the project's main office, where it will be maintained. Counselling staff, supervisory personnel, and the project director will have access to all collected data. However, only the project director, or his duly authorized representative, may divulge any confidential data contained in an offender's file without first having received the offender's signed permission. This procedure will not apply to confidential information transmitted to the offices of the prosecutor and/or juvenile court.

Data Validation

All required data will be verified by appropriate counselling staff. Periodic supervisory review will serve as a double check on the data validation process.

REFERENCES

Albanese, Robert, *Management: Toward Accountability for Performance,* Richard D. Auchincloss, Publisher, 1975. This text provides a general discussion of goals and their importance to management. The emphasis is on control and accountability.

Etzioni, Amitai, *Modern Organizations,* New York: Prentice Hall, 1964, p. 7. Reviews of all of the key elements of modern organizations. Analyzes the parameters of organizational evaluation.

LEAA, *Planning and Designing for Juvenile Justice,* Washington: U. S. Government Printing Office, August, 1972. An understandable guide to systems planning in juvenile justice. Provides a step by step approach to planning.

Leach, Edmund, "A Plan for Meaningful Justice," *Crime Prevention Review,* October, 1974, p. 67. Presents a comprehensive program for providing justice to all segments of society.

LaBreton, Preston, and Dale Henning, *Planning Theory,* New Jersey: Prentice Hall, 1961. One of the earlier texts on planning. It reviews planning at all levels of the organization. Discusses in detail—need determination, selection of alternatives, and organizational planning.

MITRE Corporation. *Evaluation in Criminal Justice Programs: Guidelines and Examples,* Washington, D. C.: Law Enforcement Assistance Administration, National Institute of Law Enforcement and Criminal Justice, May, 1973. Contains material of the quantification of goals and objectives. Discusses the relationship of goals to objectives.

City of Palo Alto, *Municipal Service Handbook,* Palo Alto, California, 1973. Provides all the rules, regulations and guidelines affecting the employees of the City of Palo Alto.

Whisenand, Paul, and Fred Ferguson, *The Managing of Police Organizations,* New York: Prentice-Hall, 1973. Contains a discussion of values and goals as it relates to the police agency. Presents the current thinking relating management to the behavioral sciences.

Chapter Objectives

1. Acquaints the reader with the relationship of data collection to the planning process.
2. Provides an awareness of the techniques of data collection.
3. Promotes an understanding of data analysis in a criminal justice environment.
4. Describes specific techniques of data collection.
5. Briefly describes data availability.
6. Describes three classifications of data collection.
7. Presents the properties of the four levels of measurement.
8. Introduces the reader to the data requirements for the criminal justice system.

3
Data Collection and Analysis

The previous chapters have laid the basic framework for criminal justice planning. Simon has noted that is not new to private enterprise (Simon, 1963, pp. 1-3) and has discussed it by using programmed and nonprogrammed decisions.

Anthony, in his text on Planning and Control (Anthony, 1965, p. 15) distinguishes the framework in terms of strategic planning, management control and operational control.

The point of developing a framework is that it sets the parameters on the types and techniques to be used in data collection. This chapter will discuss the techniques that a criminal justice planner should be aware of and the type of analysis that the planner can perform. Before that can take place a planner should have an idea of the data currently available.

Data Availability

In the field of criminal justice there is a mystique and unawareness about the types of data obtainable. Agencies are aware of the FBI's Uniform Crime Reports, giving annual figures for index crimes, clearance data on index crimes, etc. However, beyond this there appears to be a void concerning sources from which data may be drawn. One notable source that has compiled criminal justice data from a myriad of compilations is the Source Book of Criminal Justice Statistics (U.S. Dept. of Justice, LEAA, National Criminal Justice Information and Statistics Service, 1974).

This document provides data on state and county criminal justice systems. Figure III-1 illustrates the types of data

Major Sections	Data Compiled
Criminal Justice System by agency, i.e. law enforcement, adjudicative, and corrections.	• Agency distribution. • Organization. • Employment and expenditure data.
Public Attitudes	• Attitudes toward crime, adjudication process, and use of drugs.
Known Offenses	• Surveys, estimates of victimization, estimates of business loss from crime. • Offenses known to non-police agencies. • Victim-offender characteristics.
Arrest Statistics	• Number arrested. • Clearance rates. • Number of cases, appeals, disposition. • Conviction rates, sentencing data.
Corrections	• Probation frequency, caseload sizes. • Inmates of institutions. • Paroles, characteristics of parolees, violations.

FIGURE III-1. Sourcebook of Criminal Justice.

contained in the sourcebook. Another excellent source for date and study is provided by the National Criminal Justice thesaurus, published by LEAA. An overview of what is contained in the thesaurus is found in the Resource Section at the end of this chapter.

Further, many states and some planning regions are enacting what is known as Offender Based Transactional Statistics. This system provides a tracking of the defendant from point of arrest through disposition, either by exit from the system or commitment to correction. These statistics are valuable to the planner in aiding him to:

• Assess how the criminal justice system operates to process offenders.
• Determine the time it takes to process individuals.
• Determine the "clients" of the criminal justice system.
• Determine and construct profiles of offenders and crime types.

Other sources of data might come from the following:

- Statistical Abstract of the United States
- Municipal Year Book (ICMA)
- The County and City Data Book
- Local records, internal management reports and records, planning department reports and records
- State records

Data Requirements for Criminal Justice

A report entitled "Criminal Justice System" prepared for the National Advisory Commission on Criminal Justice Standards and Goals noted that the biggest obstacle to improvement of the criminal justice system has been the lack of data regarding its present operation. Recommendations of the commission are as follows:

> All criminal justice agencies, those with operational responsibilities and those with planning or policy responsibilities, require substantial data to function properly as a part of the overall criminal justice system. In general, criminal justice agencies require information on the events that initiate and terminate criminal justice processes; on people (suspects, victims, offenders, etc.) who are relevant to the operation of the criminal justice system; on property (particularly when stolen or associated with a criminal event); and on the operation of the agencies themselves.
>
> The needs for information tend to be related either to a single item or record or to a group of records. In the first instance, the information needed generally is considered to be operational information where the requester seeks data, such as the history of involvement with criminal justice or property status, to assist him in performing his duties.
>
> The second category, where the request is for aggregate information from multiple records, is of primary use in management. Since management of criminal justice involves planning, organizing, directing, and evaluating activities, most of the information needs are statistical in nature. Here the statistical characteristics of groups of data are used to assist criminal justice managers in the decisionmaking processes to enable them to operate their respective agencies more efficiently and to meet stated crime reduction goals.

The raw data needed for both operational and management purposes often comes from a common source. The report of a crime, for example, is used by investigators in their operational followup to the event, and also is used in the generation of crime statistics for management purposes. Thus, although the users of information may vary, there is a common single source for much of the raw data needed in all components of the criminal justice system.

Police, courts, and correctional agencies each have specific information needs. However, there are several categories of data that should serve all criminal justice agencies. Three categories now are being developed under high priority by the Law Enforcement Assistance Administration and various state and local agencies to improve the general state of knowledge. These system-wide needs include a basic criminal history record; statistics about the activities of the system with respect to offenders, and crime occurrence data.

A criminal history record is a major thread in tying the criminal justice system together. It shows, as no other document or record does, the actions of the total system on individuals. It describes the actions of police agencies, judicial and supportive agencies and all correctional components. Improved processing or computerization of these records offers great promise in the attempt to upgrade the performance of the criminal justice system and to improve the administration of justice.

Closely allied to the need for ciminal history data for a given offender is the need for aggregate data on the way offenders are processed through the system. The demand for offender-based transaction statistics has become more acute as planning and legislative actions result in redefinition of the operation of the criminal justice system.

The evaluation of whether a part of the system is meeting its basic objectives must have its roots in the statistics describing the passage of offenders through the system. In addition to the historical data made a part of an individual's criminal history records, statistical requirements include data dealing with the passage of time and other aspects of the handling of offender workload. It is this system of offender-based transaction statistics that describes the relationship of the components of criminal justice to each other.

A key element in an offender-based transaction system is the disposition of the offender's case as it moves from one component of criminal justice to the next. That is, the data must include the disposition or other action taken by the police, the action taken by the courts, and the action of various correctional cycles through which an offender passes. Also critical in this statistical system is the identification of the point at which the offender leaves the system.

Another major system-wide need is data regarding the crime itself. Although police managers may have more immediate need for thorough and comprehensive data on the occurrence of crime, planners involved in all aspects of criminal justice require better estimates of the variations in crime rates and the characteristics of criminal events in order to anticipate workload. Legislators and planning agencies that participate in the setting of policies regarding the handling of criminal events also require comprehensive data on the nature of crime. The present system of crime reporting, as conducted by the FBI in the Uniform Crime Reporting Program (UCR), is the minimal starting point in collecting the data needed by these agencies.

In addition to describing the complete set of events defined as crimes, a need exists for data on the victims of crimes. As the role of victims in crime has come into focus, the need to know about the nature of a victim and his involvement in a crime has become increasingly apparent, and actions are under-way to correct this lack.

Data on victims is needed for all crimes. Statistics based on crimes known to the police, while extremely valuable, cannot provide all the facts necessary to assess and deal with the crime problem in the United States. The most serious problem stems from the fact that, for one reason or another, many people fail to report crimes to the police.

Further, a great deal of critical information concerning the victim is not recorded at the time the offense report is completed. The already heavy reporting burden on the investigating officer, and the fact that much of the information is irrelevant to the solution of the case at hand, preclude capturing the requisite data. Information on the circumstances surrounding the event, the general environment in which the event occurred, the number and characteristics of the victims, the characteristics of the offenders, if known, and other strategic information for both reported and unreported crimes must be available if rational steps are to be taken to reduce crime.

One method of systematically obtaining that data is through general population surveys. Such surveys have become accepted methods of determining, with relative accuracy, the level of reported and unreported crime as well as its characteristics. The National Criminal Justice Information and Statistics Service has developed a survey unit, the National Crime Panel, to provide national data and data for the central cities of the largest metropolitan areas.

Although general population surveys are costly for widespread use by local agencies, victim studies still are needed. Victim survey techniques can use recent crimes reported to the police as a basis of a sample. Surveys using crimes reported to the police will not provide any concrete information as to the level of crime, but will provide detailed information about the victims, the events, and their characteristics.

These three information needs—criminal history, offender-based transaction statistics, and crime data—have application for more than a single component of the criminal justice system. There is another major requirement of criminal justice agencies—the need for internal management information. As the cost of operating the criminal justice system increases and tax revenues become more scarce, agencies are under increasing pressure to operate at maximum efficiency. Managers therefore require data that enable them to measure performance and to make maximum use of available resources.

The information included in this requirement is primarily of interest to the individual agency, although the categories of data include resources available (people and equipment) and fiscal data. The system, whether automated or not, must help the manager allocate resources. In police agencies, allocation concentrates on patrol forces. In courts, the problem includes jury utilization and court personnel allocation. In corrections, allocation deals with facilities and people.

The system also must support resource planning and budget analysis, personnel administration, inventory control, and other typical management information functions. These are all important elements in agency administration, but this particular work assumes that this problem is largely one each agency must face as a part of general management, and that it is more important to deal with those requirements that satisfy the operational and interagency data needs.

There are, in addition to these common needs, particular needs faced by police, courts, and corrections. Here the criminal justice planner must be able to identify the problem, collect and analyze the data, and make his recommendations in the form of solutions. The remainder of this chapter will concentrate on the methods that the planner might use to collect data that is not readily available: e.g., data needed to evaluate a program.

Data Collection Methods

The methods of data collection for the criminal justice system can be categorized into three classifications:

- Baseline Data Collection
- Field Data Collection
- Experimental Data Collection

Each of these methods has a sub-set methodology to collect the data and a technique for analyzing the data. This discussion will focus on the methods and sub-sets only, since the techniques are discussed at length in Chapter IV.

The method of data collection refers to the place that data is usually collected. For example, Baseline data would involve library type of research. Field data collection would consist of collecting data that is normally not found in available documentation. Experimental data collection refers to "laboratory" type of collection efforts. An example might be to collect data on the use of stress training for police officers, with a control and experimental group of officers. Figure III-2 indicates the three classifications above as they relate to these sub-set methods. The sub-set methods refer to the means or procedures that are used to collect the data. As can be seen by the figure these include observations, questionnaires, interviews, etc.

Method	Sub Set Method (Procedures)	(Techniques)
Baseline Data Collection	Analysis of historical records, criminal justice management reports, UCR reports.	Taking notes. Descriptive or content analysis.
	Analysis of agency documents, statistical and non-statistical agency records.	Statistical compilation and manipulation.
		Graphs.
		Charts.
	Literature search for previous research or theories that would impact on the criminal justice problem defined. Research books, journals, National Criminal Justice Reference Service.	
Field Data Collection	Questionnaire	Use of attitudinal scales to measure agency performance job satisfaction, morale.
	Interview	
	Case Study	Content analysis.
	Observation	Use of opinions recording behavior.
	Expert Opinion	Delphi or other appropriate method.
Experimental	Small group study, problem solving, control groups. Program experimentation.	Use of structural experiences; pilot tests. Use of observers. Use of simulation, modeling, senarios, etc.

FIGURE III-2.   Classification of Data.

Analyzing Data

After data have been collected, they must be compiled and rearranged to make them yield the information they contain. This is the process of data analysis.

Many different processes in criminal justice are called "analysis". What type of analysis a manager/planner does depends upon the type of question that he seeks to answer as well as on the method by which he collects the data and the acuteness with which the question or hypothesis has been formulated.

A good analysis shows the important data in a clearly understandable form so the meaning is easily grasped by the reader. For example, there should be a separate table or graph for each point you are trying to make, rather than one enormous master compilation in which nothing is obvious.

The more complicated processes of analysis take place in causal- and noncausal-relationship research and in comparison research.

Regardless of what type of problem you want to work on and no matter what processes you will eventually use, your work must begin with a careful consideration of the criminal justice problem. You must define what you are trying to find out. You must ask: What information am I trying to obtain? What is the precise question to which I seek a possible answer?

It is difficult to specify a possible answer to a specific problem. It is much easier to wave your hands and in vagueness ask: "I'm interested in getting some answers about juvenile delinquency." What answers? To what questions? Do you want to know how many juvenile delinquents there are? Or whether separated parents affect the rate of juvenile delinquency? Or whether or not juvenile delinquents delight in their delinquency? Or what? Each of the above questions can still be further defined to aid the planner.

The above discussion applies to all data collection efforts. An excellent illustration of this appeared in the recent National Advisory Commission Report on Criminal Justice Standards and Goals, "Scientific Method and Research Methodology: Introduction," The Criminal Justice System (1973). Following are some excerpts from that report as they relate to building a sound research design and collecting the correct type of data. This serves as an example only, but the criminal justice planner should keep these principles in mind when developing a program or evaluating a program:

> The fundamental system of thinking and action that permeates processes of effective program evaluation is the philosophy of inquiry; or the application of the scientific method to guide observations, measurements, and evaluations of data. This

philosophy postulates the procedures and techniques of scientific research for gaining knowledge. It also proposes a certain attitude—the empirical attitude that searches for and relies on objective factual observations and evidence.

In addition to its empirical base, the scientific method is systematic. Conducted according to a comprehensive plan (the research design), it not only specifies what to observe, but looks for relationships, patterns, and order between observations. It also supplies the power of self-correction via built-in controls that help verify the reliability and validity of the data attained. "Control" means the ability to isolate and assess the fluctuation of variables which are relevant to what is being observed.

Research investigations are open, explicit and reproducible while the assumptions, values, calculations, limitations and conclusions are documented and susceptible to testing, criticism and refutation.

Every administrator within the criminal justice system should possess a working knowledge of the philosophy of the scientific method and how this method can be harnessed to enhance the process of program evaluation. Essentially the scientific method requires the following:

1. Reliance on facts. "Facts" refers to events which may be directly observed and replicated. ("Evidence" could be substituted for "facts.")

2. Use of systems analysis in comprehending complex phenomena. Analysis involves division of system or program into the specific procedures and operations for purposes of assessment, design and redesign.

3. Development of hypotheses to guide research. Hypotheses are careful explicit predictions of outcomes that can be tested against observations.

4. Depersonalization or freedom from bias and the subjectivity that characterizes common sense convictions.

5. Objective measurement. Knowledge expands in large part through the development and refinement of instruments of measurement.

6. Quantitative methods to treat data. The main concepts are operationally defined; that is, the activities performed to manipulate and measure a concept are specified in quantifiable terms. Additionally, the objective language of statistics is channeled to analyze, classify and summarize data.

Research Procedures and Principles

Use of the scientific method as a philosophy and tool for program evaluation should be guided by a set sequence of research procedures. These procedures are constructed to insure collection and self-correction of data to unify the data into objective conclusions. Although defined separately for clarity, some procedures overlap and often proceed simultaneously. These procedures are:

- Statement of the problem including some history about why resolution is important. Defining the problem in a way conducive to experimentation is as essential as searching for the solution.
- Review of the literature and previous experience to gather information about alternative strategies and solutions—what has been accomplished.
- Development of hypotheses to guide the research and test results of the program.
- Selection of the setting, including time schedule, staff and budget.
- Determination of the research design or overall plan to collect and analyze the data. Careful planning is mandatory at this point so that observations and measurements actually address objectives and produce suitable feedback.
- Selection of the population to be evaluated and the sample to participate in the experiment.
- Identification of data to be collected plus design or selection of data collection instruments: questionnaires, examinations, interviews, observations.
- Implementation of the experiment and collection of data according to the preset design and time schedule.
- Statistical analysis and interpretation of results.
- Written report.

Constructed to provide objective data and conclusions about results of ongoing and proposed programs, evaluation may be said to equal research. And when guided by the requirements attendant to the scientific method, evaluation produces feedback for more knowledgeable allocation of resources.

Use of Experimentation

Before installation of a proposed program, a research investigation should be conducted to determine the relationship of the proposed program's output to overall agency objectives and needs. The system to evaluate the program should be designed and tested concomitantly with conceptualization and development of the program. This is often referred to as survey research. The following are steps a planner should be aware of and use as a guide:

1. Carefully decide what is to be found out, and write down the general questions to have answered.
2. Develop a questionnaire or interview format that will answer the research questions.
3. Randomly select and collect data.
4. Check the reliability and validity of the survey.
5. Summarize and tabulate data, i.e. means, mode standard deviation, etc.
6. Examine data and attempt to derrive answers to the research questions.

Results of the investigation should identify significant program components such as inputs, processes, constraints and objectives—what the program expects to produce in terms of immediate and long-range goals.

The research should evaluate the measures of effectiveness—quantitative and qualitative—that can be monitored to appraise the direction and progress of the program toward the stated objectives.

Decisions about the value of a program depend on the methodology and measurement of accomplishments to distinguish program effects from effects of other forces interlacing the environment—to isolate what happened as a result of the program from what would have happened anyway.

Principles of experimental research provide the basis for estimating the amount and direction of program effects. Experimentation utilizes empirical tests of hypotheses in a manner that strives to exclude or correct extraneous influences, thus clearing the way for reasonable inferences concerning factors of significance. In basic outline, experimentation does the following:

- Exposes an experimental group to the experimental treatment program which is the independent variable symbolized as X. An example of X might be stress training for law enforcement officers.
- Does not expose the control group to the independent variable.
- Compares both groups on the dependent variable, symbolized as Y. In keeping with the above example, Y might be field performance. In this example the purpose of the experiment would be to evaluate the effect of stress training on field performance.

Through the use of quantitative and qualitative criteria, measurements of effectiveness, and methods of statistical analysis, research experimentation compares outcomes for the control and experimental groups that were randomly selected from a common population. Random selection means that each person in the population experienced an equal opportunity to be selected for either group. The experimental program (independent variable) is applied to the experimental group and withheld from the control group. Because subjects were assigned at random (or matched on relevant traits, then randomly assigned), the groups may be considered comparable and observed differences credited to the experimental program.

A primary concern of experimentation is to seek out possible casual relationships between significant variables. These relations are made to surface by subjecting the data to statistical tests of significance. From the findings, the administrator may infer with known degrees of confidence how X affects Y. For example, he will be able to estimate whether X and Y vary together in some correlated fashion; or whether X causes or leads to Y; and, if so, with what frequency.

Independent	Dependent
if — — — — — — — — → (then)	
variable	variable

FIGURE III-3. Single Variable Experimental Design.

This description of experimentation, popularly considered as the scientific method, contains these core components: dependent variable, independent variable, careful ignoring of irrelevant variables, and careful control of other relevant variables. When properly conducted, it leads to the "if-then" statement (Figure III-3): that is, if this is the case, then that will happen. If frustration, then aggression. The then part of the statement houses the dependent variable whose effects are dependent upon how the investigator manipulates the if (independent) variable. . . .

The report goes on to state that data can be used in many forms but in experimentation it is reduced to numbers so that the mass of observations can be analyzed and evaluated. The rules selected to assign numbers to observations are the criteria that define the level of measurement, the numerical scale employed in the experiment, and the statistical operations used to analyze the data.

The four levels of measurement in their ascending order of power are the nominal, ordinal, interval and ratio scales. The higher the level, the more information there is about the phenomenon. For this reason, investigators should strive to use the highest possible level of measurement in a given situation.

Administrators should possess a working knowledge of the properties and uses of the four levels of measurement. Briefly, they are:

- The nominal or classificatory scale refers to the simplest level where numbers are used to distinguish persons or traits. Example: male-female; married-single. The essence of this scale is classification. There is no numerical value attached to the classificatory scales and they do not represent a value or amount of anything. Nominal measurements rest on two rules: all members of a set are assigned the same number; and each set has a different number.

- The ordinal scale should be used when the observations can be related and rank-ordered into possessing "greater than" or "less than" amounts of the attribute under study. This scale distinguishes one object from another and also tells whether the object contains more or less of the trait than other objects in the set. The scale provides no information on the amount of difference between objects. It also possesses no absolute quantities, nor equal intervals between the numbers. For example, because the numbers are equally spaced on the scale does not mean that the underlying properties they represent are equally spaced also. Radical differences in correspondence may go undetected. The ordinal scale possesses no true zero point so there is no way to detect when the object contains none of the property.

- Interval scale refers to a level of measurement that should be used when the distance between any two numbers is equal and of known size. This scale possesses all characteristics of the nominal and ordinal scales plus numerically equal distances. This means that equal distances on the scale depict equal distances in what is being measured.

- The ratio scale is the most sophisticated level and one rarely attained by social research. It possesses all properties of the other scales plus absolute zero at its point of origin. This addition enables application of all arithmetic operations to data.

This scale is used for physical measurements such as length, time, and weight. With its absolute zero, statements of ratios are meaningful; for example, a 6-inch line is twice as long as a 3-inch line.

Some form of a ratio scale should be used when the investigator needs to state relationships between variables as products: for example, an individual's preference for a given

Scale	Properties	Examples
Nominal	Classification	Male-Female, True-False
Ordinal	Classification + order	H.S. grade level, height of individuals.
Interval	Classification + order + equal units	IQ Scores, Income in Dollars.
Ratio	Classification + order + equal units + absolute zero.	Can Add & Subtract Scores, Compare Scores.

FIGURE III-4. Properties of the Four Levels of Measurement.

event equals the product of its utility to him and his expectation of it happening.

In the process of program evaluation, much time is devoted to observing. Observations supply the raw material for testing the hypotheses. The first step in reducing the mass of data into a format understandable by the human mind is to redefine the observations into a numerical form that can be handled statistically. This is done by the measurement method: and the degree of information achieved is dependent on the level of measurement utilized.

Properties of the four levels are summarized by Figure III-4. Each ascending level contains properties of the lower levels, and the higher the level, the more information is available.

Isomorphism

Measurement procedures should be isomorphic (similar in form) to the central features of the variables under study and to the practical world of the organization.

The most important choice and the first step in measurement procedures identifies what concepts to measure and then defines the activities that will set them in motion. This choice is critical because many measurements can be meaningless: elaborate, precise techniques that define trivia are worse than useless because of wasted resources. How can this be avoided? By tying measurements to reality. That is, by actuating concepts, defining the rating scale, and defining the rules of correspondence so that the outcome—the measurements —reasonably connect variables to the lived-in-world.

When this connection holds, the measurement process is isomorphic: that is, identity or similarity of form, which is the ultimate goal of the measurement procedure.

Steps in the Measurement Process

Any measurement process should include at least these steps:

1. Determine the objective—the purpose of the program. Without clear objectives, it is impossible to set standards to evaluate performance.
2. Decide relevant factors. These are easy to define when dealing with physical systems: not so with social systems where evaluation routinely proceeds with limited information.
3. Select key indicators of factors; indicators which are quantifiable or in some way translatable to numerical ratings.
4. Select or construct (a) the measuring method and (b) the measuring unit. For example, in measuring police field performance, the measuring method might include completion of a five-point ordinal-scaled questionnaire by first line supervisors. The measuring unit is the quantity or amount of the concerned concept contained in the observation. This unit is usually fixed arbitrarily and standardized for all observations. In the example of field performance after establishing a standard unit the investigator would estimate how many units of, say, "initiative" were "expressed" by each subject.
5. Apply the measuring unit to the concept to be measured according to the preset rules of correspondence. This step starts the main action of measurement by translating the observation to a number (the number of units).
6. Examine the data with appropriate methods of statistical analysis.

7. Evaluate effectiveness of the measurement process by assessing its contributions to the program's objectives.

Measurement prescribes certain processes involving an observer, an observation, and some form of measuring instrument, the combination of which produces a number (the measure) that stands for the observation. The overall process follows certain requirements decided initially and set forth in the research design.

Data Collection Instruments and Techniques

Data collection instruments should portray systematic and standardized procedures for obtaining information. They are extensions of measurement theory in that they serve the technical purpose of translating variables into numbers.

Categorized by their degree of directness, the main instruments and techniques include interviews, questionnaires, direct observations, participant observations, analysis of records, and projective techniques.

When drafting an interview or questionnaire schedule, these criteria should guide selection of its contents:

- Is the question akin to the research problem? Except for identifying data, all items should elicit information that can be used to test the hypotheses.
- Is the question appropriate? Some inquiries need an unstructured, open-ended question such as opinions, intentions, and attitudes. Others can be better collected by concise closed questions such as the choice between alternative events.
- Is the question loaded, does it suggest an answer? These questions threaten validity. Example: Asking whether a person visited his police department during their last open house may receive many "false positive" replies because of the question's high degree of social desirability.

- Does the question ask for information that the respondent does not possess? To offset this absence, "information filter" questions should be used. That is, describe the thrust of the question before asking for an opinion. Example: describing a new method to expedite court cases before asking for a value judgment.
- Is the question weighted with social desirability? People tend to answer in ways that enhance their self-image, and may respond with what they think they should believe rather than what they do.
- Questions that call for personal information should be posed after rapport is established.
- Are the questions clear? To aid clarity, the questioner should: limit each question to one idea; avoid ambiguous expressions, long questions, and words with double meanings; pose the question in a clear context, unless ambiguity is used deliberately to draw out different viewpoints; specify the time, place, and context the respondent is expected to assume; preface unfamiliar or complicated questions with an explanatory paragraph or illustrations; and recount the question according to the respondent's experience rather than in generalities.

The sequence and administration of schedules can strongly sway answers. These guidelines should be considered when designing the instrument:

- For a given topic, begin with a general question followed by more specific ones. This harmonizes with the funnel technique of leading off with broad open-ended inquiries, then narrowing down to specifics.
- The order should be logical and avoid abrupt transition in issues. Possible orderings: easy to difficult; chronological; general to specific; special locations for sensitive questions; or random locations to eliminate researcher bias.
- Questions about controversial issues may antagonize the respondent and taint all subsequent answers. These should be dealt with last.

- All schedules should be pretested for clarity and validity on a group similar to the research sample.
- Some questions should be repeated to build in measures of reliability. If the person answers a question one way at the beginning and another way later on, the question may not be reliable.
- Avoid initial questions that disclose the purpose of the research. In trying to be helpful, the subject may sacrifice candor.
- The schedule should be reviewed by persons knowledgeable about the research problem.

Interviewers should be carefully selected and trained. Rewarding results depend on the skill of interviewers. Their screening should concentrate on at least these criteria:

- Maturity, intelligence and poise. These traits encourage cooperation and contacts conducive to candid, truthful answers.
- Ability to interact easily with people, communicate importance of the experiment, and gain cooperation.
- Ability to perceive and record responses objectively.
- Noncommittal, nonjudgmental attitude and demeanor.

Observation is the oldest technique for collecting data. It is handy when individuals do not choose to talk or when observing a particular situation or event:

- Data should be recorded as it occurs.
- To escape the volumes of data that accompany ambiguity of purpose, observations should address specific issues.
- Observations apply to overt actions only. They should not be used to evaluate personal perceptions such as beliefs, values, and feelings.
- To enhance reliability, at least two persons should observe the same event.

Participant-observation unveils behavior ordinarily shielded from research. In addition the report concludes:

- Certain ethical questions arise by the clandestine nature of this activity. The participant observer may be cleared by the agency while those in the concerned group remain unaware of his actual status.
- This technique should be carefully weighed for its cost-benefit ratio. The participant-observer's behavior will influence the actions and direction of the concerned group.

The structure and processes of research and measurement engage in a mutual interplay of influence with the instruments and methods to collect the data. Research problems dictate the instruments, but the instruments—their availability, feasibility, and relevance—also shade the selection and solution of problems. Many problems defy solution because, as yet, instruments do not exist to collect the data.

Summary

This chapter has introduced the planner to some basic considerations in data collection and analysis. Critical to all programs in criminal justice is the desire to evaluate their effectiveness. The basis for this evaluation is data collection and analysis of a hypothesis. The intent of this chapter has been to expand the awareness of the reader as to the importance and use of data collection and analysis.

This was accomplished by discussing data availability in the criminal justice system and briefly discussing the data requirements needed for criminal justice. Data collection and analysis considerations were presented and consideration was given to levels of measurement and the classification of data collection.

Topics for Discussion

1. Discuss each of the three classifications of data collection.
2. Discuss how experimentation can be used in the criminal justice environment.

3. Discuss the steps in the measurement process.

4. Discuss the criteria used in guiding the selection of the content for a questionnaire.

5. Discuss the steps that should be taken in survey research. Explain their relevance to the scientific method.

RESOURCE

NATIONAL CRIMINAL JUSTICE THESAURUS*

The NATIONAL CRIMINAL JUSTICE THESAURUS contains various listings of terms used to index the literature in the National Criminal Justice Reference Service (NCJRS) data base and to store and retrieve the information about that literature for users of the service. Term selection has been based in large part on the vocabulary of the authors of documents entering the NCJRS system, on the frequency in the literature and the language of the user community.

Definitions and Conventions

Term Levels—The Thesaurus employs two levels of word association terms called subject and content indicators.

- Subject indicators are general terms covering the broad topics of the literature.
- Content indicators are specific terms covering the detailed substance of the documents. Terms which identify organizations and geographic locations are also included in this level of indicators.

Term Groups—A two-tiered hierarchic arrangement of terms has been established to assist indexers and users. Each

---

* Source: *The National Criminal Justice Thesaurus,* United States Department of Justice, Law Enforcement Assistance Administration, National Criminal Justice Reference Service, Washington, D.C. 20530.

content indicator is assigned to the subject indicator that, in NCJRS use, reflects the most common relationship of the terms. However, the relationships are dynamic and all valid indicators may be used interchangeably in any combination of subject and/or content indicators.

Code Numbers—Codes are assigned to each indicator for internal NCJRS use. Codes consist of a leading alpha character followed by a dash and a series of numbers. An S-xxxx code identifies a subject indicator, C-xxxx identifies a content indicator, and G-xxxx identifies a geographic content indicator.

Term Length—Terms are limited to 42 characters, including spaces, but not including code numbers.

Punctuation—A minimum of punctuation is employed and periods, commas, semi-colons, and colons are excluded whenever possible.

Grammatical Form—Thesaurus terms appear in the noun form. Verbs are not normally used although, in some cases, gerunds are used as substitutes for nouns, e.g., SENTENCING.

Singular vs Plural—The singular form is usually used for comprehensive or mass nouns (those which answer how much?) and for specific processes, e.g., BAIL REFORM, not BAIL REFORMS. The plural form is used when the entry is a count noun (one that indicates how many?), e.g., SUPPORT SERVICES.

Direct Entry—Indicators consisting of more than one word are listed for direct entry in their natural rather than inverted form, e.g., AIRCRAFT SECURITY, not SECURITY, AIRCRAFT.

Abbreviations and Acronyms—Those in common use in the law enforcement and criminal justice community are used; however, abbreviations or acronyms not commonly used are avoided because of multiple meanings. Parenthetic expressions are used to clarify term ambiguity, e.g., WALES (WASH AREA LAW ENFORCEMENT SYSTEM).

Scope Notes—Specific use of terms in the NCJRS system is explained in scope notes which restrict and limit terms within the context of the indexing system. These "definitions" are presented in Section VI, and cover all subject indicators and selected content indicators requiring clarification of use, e.g.,

POLICE ORGANIZATION: Factors related to the orderly arrangement of resources available for the most effective operation of law enforcement activities.

USE Terms—These terms are not valid indicators. They are included in the alphabetic listing to direct the indexer or searcher from invalid synonyms to valid indicators, e.g., INEBRIATION, USE DRUNKENNESS. In this example, INEBRIATION is the *USE* term. DRUNKENNESS is the valid indicator.

Term Sequence—The ordering of indicators into alphabetic sequence is based on computer sorting order.

Organization

The National Criminal Justice Thesaurus is organized in six sections:

- Section I is an alphabetic listing of the subject indicators.
- Section II is a hierarchic listing of the subject indicators and their associated content indicators. This section is arranged alphabetically by subject, and by content indicators within each subject group.
- Section III is an alphabetic list of both subject and content indicators and includes *USE* terms.
- Section IV is an alphabetic list of geographic locations which is presented in two parts: 1) the several states of the United States and associated counties and cities; 2) other countries and regions. Codes assigned these content indicators are based on Federal Information Standards Publication 6-1, June 1970. These indicators appear only in this section of the Thesaurus.
- Section V is an alphabetic listing of content indicators covering organization names used in indexing the literature.
- Section VI presents the scope notes, alphabetically by indicator, which explain NCJRS use of the terms. In

Sections I through III an asterisk precedes each indicator which has been scope noted.

Use of the Thesaurus

Most NCJRS users submit requests for information searches of the data base in natural language without reference to the NCJ Thesaurus. Many make their inquiries by telephone or in person, while others submit requests in letter form. All "natural language" inquiries are analyzed by NCJRS Referral Specialists and structured for computer retrieval of the information desired. Because of Referral Specialist familiarity with both the data base and the related Thesaurus terms, the "natural language" request will normally obtain the most effective results in the least amount of time.

General guidance for the preparation of requests for information searches of the NCJRS data base is presented here for those users who desire to structure their own search requests using Thesaurus terms.

- Documents entered in the NCJRS data base are indexed using the valid indicators, definitions, and conventions contained in this Thesaurus. The index terms topically reflect the data base content.
- To insure proper usage of these terms, the user should refer to the scope notes in Section VI, which explain NCJRS use of the terms.
- If the user has already identified the subject of his inquiry and the key words related to his inquiry, he should search the alphabetic listing of all indicators in Section III to locate corresponding NCJRS terms.
- If the user has not identified the subject of his inquiry, the listing of subject indicators in Section I may assist him to do so.
- If the user has not identified key words or specific indicators which relate to his inquiry, the heirarchical grouping of indicators in Section II may assist him to do so.

- When searching Section III, if the user cannot locate NCJRS terms to directly correspond to the key words of his inquiry, he may produce such a match by combining NCJRS terms.
- For ease of retrieval, selection of indicators included in the National Criminal Justice Thesaurus is based on the application of logical coordination of the terms *AND, OR, NOT.*
- The use of the *AND* coordinator instructs the computer to select documents which contain coverage of the terms separated by the *AND,* i.e., POLICE RECRUIT *AND* EDUCATIONAL LEVELS will call up *only* those documents with content coverage of *both* terms. Documents containing only one of the terms will not be selected.
- The *OR* coordinator obtains the opposite result of the *AND* coordinator. The use of *OR* retrieves documents which contain coverage of *either* of the terms separated by the *OR,* i.e., FOOT PATROL *OR* MOTOR PATROL will call up all documents with content coverage of FOOT PATROL *OR* MOTOR PATROL, as well as all documents containing coverage of both these indicators.
- The use of *NOT* excludes information from the search results which is not desired by the user. The *NOT* coordinator is normally used as a secondary factor to eliminate unwanted information appearing in initial search results; however, it may also be used to eliminate information from broad subject terms, i.e., CRIMINOLOGY *NOT* FORENSIC MEDICINE.

SECTION I
SUBJECT INDICATORS

CODE   INDICATOR

S—0003   ALCOHOLISM
S—0004   BAIL AND BOND
S—0005   BEHAVIORAL AND SOCIAL SCIENCE
S—0075   CIVIL RIGHTS

CODE	INDICATOR
S—0018	CLASSIFICATION OF CRIME
S—0072	CLASSIFICATION OF OFFENDERS
S—0010	COMMUNICATIONS (DATA)
S—0077	COMMUNICATIONS (VISUAL)
S—0078	COMMUNICATIONS (VOICE)
S—0076	COMMUNICATIONS EQUIPMENT
S—0079	COMMUNITY BASED CORRECTIONS (ADULT)
S—0080	COMMUNITY BASED CORRECTIONS (JUVENILE)
S—0081	COMMUNITY INVOLVEMENT
S—0011	COMMUNITY RELATIONS
S—0015	CORRECTIONAL INSTITUTIONS (ADULT)
S—0082	CORRECTIONAL INSTITUTIONS (JUVENILE)
S—0105	CORRECTIONAL MANAGEMENT
S—0071	COSTS OF CRIME
S—0016	COURT MANAGEMENT AND OPERATION
S—0083	COURT STRUCTURE
S—0084	CRIME CAUSES
S—0021	CRIME DETERRENCE AND PREVENTION
S—0085	CRIMINAL INVESTIGATION
S—0023	CRIMINALISTICS
S—0001	CRIMINOLOGY
S—0054	DEFENSE SERVICES
S—0031	DOMESTIC RELATIONS
S—0087	DRUG INFORMATION
S—0042	DRUG TREATMENT
S—0027	EDUCATION
S—0088	EXPLOSIVES AND WEAPONS
S—0089	FINANCIAL MANAGEMENT
S—0034	GAMBLING
S—0035	INDIAN AFFAIRS
S—0036	INFORMATION SYSTEMS
S—0090	INFORMATION SYSTEMS SOFTWARE
S—0091	JAILS
S—0038	JUDICIAL PROCESS
S—0092	JUVENILE COURT
S—0040	JUVENILE DELIQUENCY
S—0041	LAWS AND STATUTES
S—0045	ORGANIZED CRIME
S—0093	PARDON
S—0103	PERSONNEL ADMINISTRATION
S—0102	PLANNING AND EVALUATION

CODE	INDICATOR
S—0051	POLICE EQUIPMENT
S—0094	POLICE INTERNAL AFFAIRS
S—0048	POLICE MANAGEMENT
S—0095	POLICE ORGANIZATION
S—0096	POLICE PATROL FUNCTION
S—0097	POLICE RESOURCE ALLOCATION
S—0063	POLICE TRAFFIC FUNCTION
S—0101	PRISON DISORDERS
S—0053	PROBATION AND PAROLE (ADULT)
S—0098	PROBATION AND PAROLE (JUVENILE)
S—0060	PROSECUTION
S—0099	PUBLIC INFORMATION AND EDUCATION
S—0073	REFERENCE MATERIAL
S—0104	REHABILITATION AND TREATMENT
S—0056	RESEARCH AND DEVELOPMENT
S—0058	RIOT CONTROL AND URBAN DISORDERS
S—0002	SECURITY SYSTEMS
S—0061	STATISTICS
S—0086	STUDENT DISORDERS
S—0100	SUPPORT SERVICES
S—0064	TRAINING
S—0043	VICTIMLESS CRIME

REFERENCES

Anthony, Robert N., *Planning and Control Systems: A Framework for Analysis,* Boston: Harvard Business School, 1965. Provides the reader with a clear understanding of the planning and control mechanizms in organizations.

Lundgren, Earl, *Organizational Management—Systems and Processes,* San Francisco: Canfield Press, 1974. A general management text, emphasis is on the behavioral systems approach.

National Advisory Commission on Criminal Justice Standards and Goals, *Criminal Justice System,* Washington, D.C.: U.S. Government Printing Office, 1973. This report looks at the various components of the criminal justice system. It presents a true "Systems Approach" to examining the system.

Simon, Herbert, *Administrative Behavior,* New York: Free Press, 1965. Discusses decision making in organizations. Presents a clear understanding of administrative behavior and associated problems.

Simon, Herbert, *A Framework for Decision Making,* Proceedings of a Symposium on Decision Theory, Athens, Ohio: Ohio University, 1963, pp. 1-3. Discusses the administrative decision making process that takes place in organizations.

Sourcebook of Criminal Justice Statistics, U.S. Department of Justice, Law Enforcement Assistance Administration, Washington, D.C.: U.S. Government Printing Office, 1974. Provides statistical data and all components of the criminal justice system. Also provides comparative data.

Chapter Objectives

1. Introduces the reader to some of the major techniques of planning.
2. Explains the use of techniques of planning in a criminal justice environment.
3. Provides practical examples of planning techniques.
4. Briefly describes the technique of content analysis.
5. Differentiates between modeling and simulations.
6. Describes statistical analysis.
7. Identifies elements of descriptive analysis.

4
Techniques of Planning

Consistent with the three methods of data collection discussed in the previous chapter, several techniques are discussed below. The list of techniques should not be construed as an exhaustive one. These are only the primary ones utilized and do overlap in their use. The techniques are listed below:

METHOD	TECHNIQUES
Baseline Data	Descriptive Analysis
Collection	Content Analysis
	Statistical Analysis
Field Data Collection	Content Analysis
	Magnitude Estimation
	Delphi & Others
	Case Study
Experimental	Structured Experiences
	Modeling
	Simulations

The Techniques of Baseline Data Collection

Three techniques specifically useful in baseline data collection will be discussed. They are:

- descriptive analysis
- content analysis
- statistical analysis

Descriptive Analysis

The use of descriptive analysis comes into play when describing an event, activity problem, etc. that has taken place. Usually one has a set of intentions they are looking at to provide a framework for description. For example, let's say we want a descriptive analysis of neighborhood team policing in a city. We could then classify our area of interest in organizational and operational elements. The elements might include:

- area served
- composition of team
- investigative responsibility
- community interaction

Each of these four factors could be described concerning effectiveness within each of the elements. Note that no judgmental characteristics should be introduced. The planner is merely describing how the program is functioning based upon the organizational and operational elements presented.

Content Analysis

From one point of view it is reasonable to call content analysis a "qualitative" technique, for the planner does not make quantitative comparisons between two or more cases. A planner may say that one police agency is "more law enforcement oriented" than another, but such a statement cannot be substantiated numerically. If you ask the planner to prove his statement quantitatively, he may reply that you are asking him to measure the unmeasurable. But content analysis is actually a method of measuring the unmeasurable—at least to some extent—and from this point of view it is sensible to call it a "quantitative" technique.

The content analysis planner sets up various classification schemes he then applies to speeches or writings. These classifications either count particular kinds of words or ideas, or they measure the amount of words or time devoted to particular ideas. An example might consist of looking for key words, in departmental general orders, providing a clue to that department's philosophy.

Content analysis can be used in studies of the mass media to determine changes in either the media or in society's perception of criminal justice. It is a formalization of techniques that have long been used informally. For example, a planner may count the number of favorable or unfavorable editorials in a county's newspaper to see how the climate toward criminal justice has changed from one period to the next, rather than merely obtaining an informal impression of the climate.

Statistical Analysis

This is probably the most widely used technique in criminal justice baseline data manipulation. The publication by the National Advisory Commission on Criminal Justice Standards and Goals (Criminal Justice System, 1973) discussed statistical analysis by stating the following:

> Methods and techniques of statistical analysis provide avenues to study and precisely describe data—its relationships, differences, and distribution. The major aim of statistics is to compare actual results with chance expectations toward the end of reducing uncertainty in decision-making. Toward this goal it treats all empirical data as chance happenings until shown to be otherwise.

To enhance our understanding of basic statistics, the following definitions are given of the most commonly used statistics:

Frequency Distribution

A frequency distribution displays a pattern of scores or numbers. For example, let's say you have just surveyed the community concerning its attitude toward the police. You developed a score for each question giving you possible scores from 10 to 100. The first step in frequency distribution is to find the highest and lowest scores. Then, arrange the other scores in descending order:

Attitude Score	Number	Frequency
100	III	3
99	II	2
98	XI	11
97	I	1
to 10		to 10

Frequency is merely a descriptive statistic telling how many times a given score occurs in data collection. These frequencies could then be depicted by a bar graph in order to facilitate interpretation.

One statistic oftentimes used in looking at criminal justice data is the measures of central tendency. These are the mean, mode and median.

Each of these are briefly discussed below:

Mean

The mean is found by dividing the sum of a series of scores (measures) by the number of scores made. Example, a supervisory promotional exam is given to four patrolmen and their scores were:

Sample	Test Score
Patrolman #1	50
Patrolman #2	60
Patrolman #3	100
Patrolman #4	100

The mean would be found by adding the four scores, and then dividing by the number of patrolmen taking the test. $310 \div 4 = 77.5$ mean score.

Median

The median is the value above which half of the test scores, measures lie. It is used when scores are badly skewed, as the median would be more indicative of performance.

Mode

The mode is the score or measure that most frequently occurs.

For a further in-depth understanding of statistical analysis and the type of statistics, an annotated bibliography is provided at the end of this chapter.

Field Data Collection

There is much overlap in using techniques as applied to data. For example, statistical techniques could be applied toward any one of the three methods discussed earlier. However, a framework was built to aid understanding. This section of the chapter will discuss the techniques that could be applied in Field data collection. They are:

- Delphi
- Delbecq
- Roundtable
- Magnitude Estimation
- Case Study

These techniques are primarily qualitative in nature allowing for human judgment to fill informational needs. Whenever possible they should be used with quantitative findings.

Delphi

The Delphi method is used to gather expert opinion. It minimizes group opinion dangers as it is a non-confrontation approach. The RAND Corporation constructed this technique for gathering expert opinions: (Dalker, 1968, and Gordon and Helmer, 1964).

> A collection of such reasons may be presented anonymously to the participants in order that they may reconsider, and possibly revise, their earlier estimate. The recycling of rounds tends to stimulate the panel experts to take into account consideration they might have neglected and to give due weight to factors they had previously dismissed as unimportant.

One recent use of this technique was utilized in forecasting criminalistics goals and requirements. (Illinois Law Enforcement Commission, 1975):

> In this case a group of eight expert panelists were put through a series of rounds to forecast future 10-year criminalistic goals. They were then put through another series of rounds to forecast future requirements based upon five criteria:
>
> - organizational structure
> - service demands
> - manpower needs
> - needed support system
> - delivery of service

It would appear that this technique has some potential for use by planners in the criminal justice area. (Delbecq, 1971, pp. 466-492).

Delbecq

This is a technique of gathering information from a group of experts. It uses components of Delphi, however, it stresses direct confrontation. The experts are gathered in a large room and then are divided into small groups. The facilitator asks everyone to spend 30 minutes defining the topic (program definition, estimation of future requirements, or whatever) on 5 × 7 cards. Group members do not discuss their cards.

At the end of 30 minutes a group recorder is randomly selected and lists one item from each group member card. The recorder writes them on a large pad without any discussion. The groups are then given a coffee break. Upon returning, each group is given ½ hour to discuss their lists. After the 30 minutes, each member of the group is given 3 × 5 cards and votes privately on which five items he considers most crucial. The votes are collected and recorded. All groups are gathered together and a brief discussion follows.

The delbecq approach was recently compared to a modified nominal group process for public sector problem solving.

For an excellent discussion of this, see (Etzel, 1974, pp. 439-446).

Roundtable

This is the traditional approach to expert opinion data gathering. A panel of experts sit around a table and directly discuss or debate the problem, solution, etc. Newman illustrates the roundtable use (Newman, 1972):

> For example, the Los Angeles Police Department has implemented the so-called Basic CAR Plan as one way of attaining the department's basic objective of helping society prevent crime through the coordinated efforts of the policeman and the people in the community. The essential idea of the Basic CAR Plan is that the officers assigned to a district meet with the citizens of the district once a month. This enables discussion of police problems between the officers and the citizens and allows for improved understanding of the nature of law enforcement needs and problems as they affect both the officers and the people being served. We asked a group of qualified individuals, specifically members of the 53rd class of the Delinquency Control Institute of the University of Southern California, to serve as experts in this exercise. The Basic CAR Plan was chosen only as an example, and no evaluation was actually intended or carried out. The experts were asked to list what they thought would be the essential criteria for evaluating the effectiveness of this program. Their response is listed under general categories and in order of importance in Figure IV-1.
>
> Note that there is considerable overlap and that many of these criteria are vague. However, by getting them out before a group they can serve as the starting point for debate.

As a method, roundtable provides a relatively quick method of achieving a group consensus. However, it also contains certain undesirable psychological factors, such as specious persuasion, the unwillingness to abandon publicly expressed opinions, and the bandwagon effect of majority opinion.

Case Study

This technique is not limited to before-and-after snapshot measures of a program. Through the use of the case study,

General	People	Officers
Crime rate	Attitude of people (youth) toward police	Officers' attitudes/understanding
Reported crime	Improved communications between community and police	Reduction in complaints on officers
Is it effective deterrent?	Plan accepted by people	Attitude of police toward plan
Does crime become a neighborhood problem or merely a simple report to police?	More or less cooperation by citizenry	Reduction in assaults on officers
What happened to clearance rate?	Persons reached from criminal element or already cooperative and working with police	Has it raised morale of department?
Number of arrests		Does officer know specific problems on his beat?
Calls for miscellaneous police services	Has it reduced racial tension	How many citizens known by name by officer on the beat?
Cost versus effectiveness	Attitude change of general public toward its role in law enforcement	Have working conditions for police improved?
	Attitude of poor in area	Are more on-sight arrests made?
	Do people relate and identify with officers in assigned area?	Has it increased efficiency of department?
*NOTE: in order of importance and/or popularity	Hostility towards police	
	Are citizens responding to meetings?	
	What type of people responding?	

*From the report by Newman, Robert and Abestone Jollee, *Evaluation Technology,* prepared for the Los Angeles Criminal Justice Planning Board, Jan., 1972.

FIGURE IV-1. List of Possible Criteria for Evaluating a Community Relations Program.

relationships between services and participants may be studied in depth in order to facilitate insights which may assist the program administrators in improving operations. Case studies are particularly important when inventive, first-of-a-kind programs are tried. Although results from an isolated case study are not generalizable to other programs, they can provide penetrating suggestions for internal program improvements. For a look at the use of case studies in criminal justice application see "Team Policing—Seven Case Studies," Police Foundation, Washington D.C., 1973.

Experimental Data Collection

The last areas to be discussed in this chapter are the myriad of techniques that fall within the framework of the Experimental Method. Some of the most popular ones will be documented in this area. The techniques are summarized as follows:

- structured experiences
- modeling
- scenarios

Structured experiences

The use of structured experiences are primarily aimed at developing learning designs to accomplish stated objectives. The experiences can cover decision making, communication, planning, etc. For example, if one were to address decision making in criminal justice, a structured experience would be developed to assess the impact of individual versus group decision making. In essence, structured experience has a well defined behavioral goal and is geared toward experimental learning.

For an in-depth look into the application of structured experiences for criminal justice consult the following text: O'Neill, Michael and Martinsen, Kai, Criminal Justice Group Training—A Facilitators Handbook, *University Associates*, La Jolla, CA, 1975. An example is provided in the Resource section of this chapter.

Modeling

The use of models help planners describe, predict or plan. Models have several components which can be discussed as they help depict a state of affairs. The specific techniques that we shall discuss under this broad heading are:

- models
- simulations
- PERT/CPM network models
- Queing Theory

Models

A model can be thought of as a pictorial representation of a problem, program, or system. In this sense, we could describe the model of the Police Adult Intake Decision Points and Alternatives (California Correctional System Intake Study, Project #1593-E, prepared for the California Department of Corrections, July, 1974), as noted in Figure IV-2. By constructing such a model we can more effectively assess and understand how a particular system works. The case in point, the police adult intake system. Models provide planners with insights into problems and provide a start for looking at alternatives and their point of impact on the system.

Simulations

Simulation can best be thought of as a technique of setting up a model or representation of a real situation and then perform variations on it. Role playing of a civil disorder is a form of simulation where we can test under a laboratory situation alternatives to crowd control, or other crime control incidents. From a criminal justice planning perspective we usually view simulation linked with computers. For example, one use of simulation using a computer might evolve around the burglary reduction process. By depicting a model we could simulate alternative measures and try to gauge their impact. It might look like Figure IV-3: (A Seminar Training Paper by Dr. Ernest Unwin, Consultant, January, 1975). It would be possible

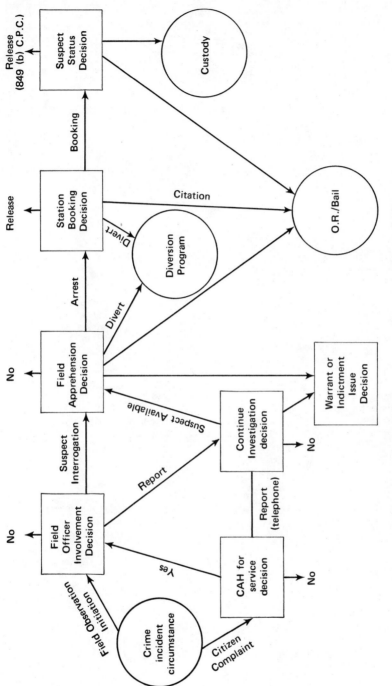

FIGURE IV-2. Police Adult Intake Decision Points and Alternatives.

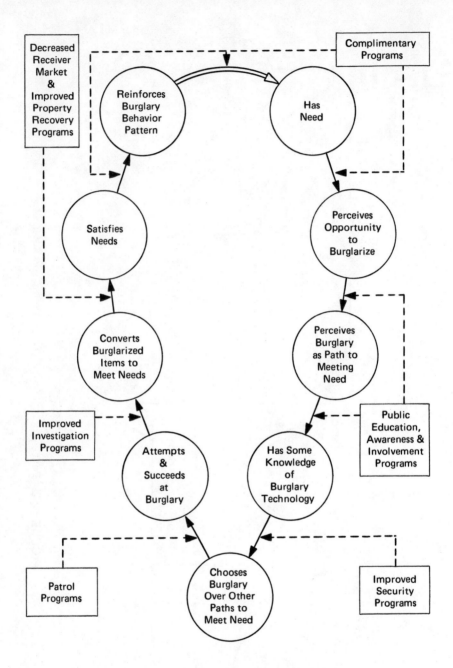

FIGURE IV-3. Interdicting the Burglary System.

by computer simulation to determine what happens if we institute a long range program. In this way it would be possible to study the effects of changes in strategies or policies on the burglary reduction process.

PERT/CPM—Dr. Peter Unsinger has emphasized that (Unsinger, 1974):

> Program evaluation and review technique (PERT) is an extension of the Gantt chart concept. Developed in 1958 by the Navy's Special Project Office and the Lockheed Aircraft Corporation for missile projects, PERT allows the planner greater flexibility than was the case with the Gantt chart. Essentially, PERT is an analytical device that shows a-1 the work necessary to achieve a stated objective/goal while at the same time allowing the planner to predict time and costs under a variety of conditions while spotlighting those uncertainties or problems that might impede, delay or frustrate the achievement of the objective/goal.
>
> The focus of PERT, is on events or activities. The event is the specific achievement or accomplishment. The activity is the work that is necessary to achieve or accomplish the event(s). The events and activities are laid out in a network. For a hypothetical Sheriff's Department communication network, a PERT network would look like Figure IV-4. The information on this simple PERT network is the same as that in Figure IV-5, Figure IV-6 and Figure IV-7 except there are no time elements. PERT must be carried further.
>
> The very first step involved in PERT is developing the network. The planner simply estimates all the events and activities that are necessary to achieve a certain goal. In the hypothetical Sheriff's Department communication center, the steps could be:
>
> a. Building—design and construct on county property.
> b. Equipment—design, set specifications, accept bids, choose, order, receive and install equipment in new building.
> c. Personnel—(1) train presently employed in new equipment; (2) train personnel transferred from other agencies in S.O. policies, etc. and in new equipment; and (3) recruit, select and train the additional personnel to be hired.

The planner can make the PERT network as simple or as complex as he desires. Often the general plan is kept simple and the appendices to the plan contain the more complex steps. For the purposes of this exercise the network will be simple and Figure IV-4 employed.

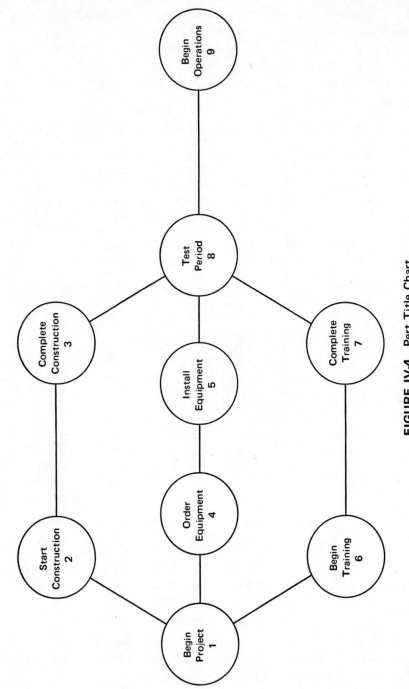

FIGURE IV-4. Pert Title Chart.

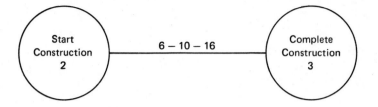

FIGURE IV-5. Pert Activity.

After the network's steps (events and activities) are laid out, the planner now calculates which events/activities can occur concurrently and which must await the completion of other steps. For instance, the hypothetical communication center cannot be tested until building, equipment and personnel are ready. The acquisition of equipment can, however, occur concurrently with either the training of personnel or the construction of the building. The desire is to have the building completed and personnel trained at the same time. That way the personnel and the building are not sitting idle—a cost with little relation to the objective/goal.

Once the logical flow of events are laid out, the planner begins to collect information on *time*. The responsibilities (i.e., contractor, equipment suppliers, trainers, etc.) are contacted and three *times* are solicited. These are their estimated *optimistic time* (to), *most likely time* (tm) and *pessimistic time* (tp). These *times* are then written onto the network in the to-tm-tp order. So if our hypothetical contractor estimates six weeks as his optimistic, ten weeks for his most likely and sixteen weeks for his pessimistic, these times would be placed on the network (activity 2-3) as indicated in Figure IV-5.

Times are solicited from each and every one of the responsibles. With all the optimistic, most likely, and pessimistic times in hand, our network now looks like Figure IV-6.

Since the times solicited are in weeks, the same unit is used throughout. The reader has probably noticed some activities have estimated times of "0-0-0" and "1-1-1". The "0-0-0" is simply a dummy activity inserted in the network to maintain the logical sequence of events. In activity 7-8, there is no time needed from those completing training to the beginning of the test of man, machine and building. The "1-1-1" of

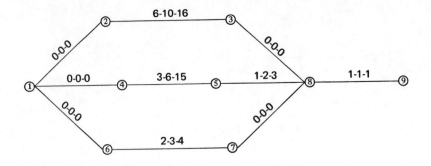

FIGURE IV-6. Pert Network.

activity 8-9 simply is the estimator allowing one week for tests—no more and no less.

All of these time estimates are fine but the planner needs to know exactly the amount of time each activity is expected to take. The expected time (te) is calculated from the to-tm-tp by using the following formula:

$$\frac{to + 4\ tp + tp}{6}$$

This formula is derived from empirical investigation and is the weighted average of all three times. There is a 50-50 chance that more or less time will be required. So the estimated time (te) for the times given by the contractor on the building would be (activity 2-3)

$$te = \frac{6 + 4(10) + 16}{6}$$

$$= \frac{6 + 40 + 16}{6}$$

$$= \frac{62}{6}$$

$$= 10.3$$

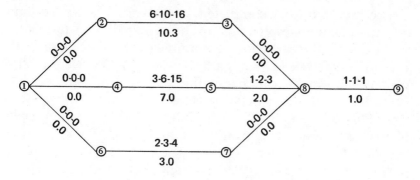

FIGURE IV-7. Pert Path Table.

The expected time from beginning construction to completion would be 10.3 weeks. Using the formula on the entire network, the network now looks like Figure IV-7.

With the optimistic/most likely/pessimistic (to-tm-tp) times as well as the expected time (te) available, the planner can easily calculate and give an inquirer an estimate of how long the plan or project will take from start to finish. By simply adding up the times in our hypothetical case and using the largest figure, the planner will be "in the ball park."

Path 1-2-3-8-9				Path 1-4-5-8-9				Path 1-6-7-8-9			
to	tm	tp	te	to	tm	tp	te	to	tm	tp	te
o	0	0	0	0	0	0	0	0	0	0	0
6	10	16	10.3	3	6	15	7	2	3	4	3
0	0	0	0	1	2	3	2	0	0	0	0
1	1	1	1	1	1	1	1	1	1	1	1
7	11	17	11.3	5	9	19	10	3	4	5	4

The answer is the expected time of 11.3 weeks and maybe as long as 19 weeks if problems develop.

Several other calculations can be made by the planner using the PERT network. If one wants to know when an event can be expected to be completed, or the earliest expected time (te), the planner simply adds up the expected times (te) along the paths. So the earliest expected time (te) for event 8 on path 1-4-5-8 is 9.0 weeks. For path 1-6-7-8 it is 3.0 weeks. The planner knows he can begin the activities of path 1-6-7-8 (te = 3.0) three weeks prior to the completion of path 1-4-5-8 (te = 90); to begin path 1-6-7-8 earlier would mean the people trained to communicate would "sit around" until the building is completed—a wasted resource. The planner may also want to know the times when each event should be begun in order to meet any "target" date for the project's completion. Called the latest allowable time (T1), the expected times (te) for each activity is subtracted back from the target date. So, if we want our hypothetical communications facility operational on July 1st, then event 5 must begin three weeks prior to that date (path 5-8-9, te 2 + 1 = 3).

CPM

The Critical Path Method (CPM) is the path with the longest times. It is determined by simply adding up all the expected times (te) of each path. The planner uses the te (expected time) since it is the weighted average. If the pessimistic time (tp) was used, then path 1-4-5-8-9 would be critical but PERT planners have found the use of expected time (te) better. Mathematicians say the odds are 100 to 1 that optimistic (to) or pessimistic (tp) will occur in reality. In our hypothetical case the critical path would then be 1-2-3-8-9 which has a total te of 11.3 weeks.

For the criminal justice system planner who must accelerate the program to meet a newer and shorter deadline than originally anticipated, this would mean concentration resources on shortening the time involved in path 1-2-3-8-9. Placing calculable resources elsewhere, while giving the idea of speeding up the project would not accomplish the purpose. The fact that activities have been speeded up on the wrong path has probably contributed to the saying "hurry up and wait." By PERT-ing out the activities, the critical path can be discovered and the "pressure" brought to bear on the right places if haste is required.

Pert/Cost

If PERT can be used to calculate times, then the planner may also want to put dollar estimates down as well. By estimating the costs, the decision-maker can put his decisions about accelerating projects in some cost perspectives.

PERT/CPM and the Planner

The management texts are full of decisions and planning models for the police/planner. As most of the men who must decide and plan will admit, a hard part of the model to meet is fully analyzing the alternatives. By using Gantt/PERT/CPM, the decision-makers and planners in criminal justice agencies can be in a better position for exploring and implementing alternatives.

Queuing theory

This is a mathematical technique which deals with problems of congestion. Queuing problems arise when service demands exceed the rate at which a required service can be provided. The applicability of queuing to the patrol force of a police department or servicing customers in a records section would present typical queuing problems. For an in-depth look into queuing application in police see Urban Police Patrol Analysis by Larsons, R.C., MIT Press, 1972.

Summary

The chapter discusses specific techniques applicable to the three methods of data collection. They are: baseline, field and experimental. The techniques covered relative to baseline are descriptive analysis, content analysis and statistical analysis. Concerning field data collection, the techniques of delphi, delbecq, roundtable, and case study are discussed. The chapter concludes with experimental and discusses the applicable techniques of structured experiences, modeling and scenarios.

Topics for Discussion

1. Describe the techniques applicable to baseline data collection, field data collection and experimental data collection.
2. Select a problem and demonstrate the use of PERT.
3. List and discuss applications in criminal justice planning that might be enhanced by the use of the Delphi Technique.
4. Discuss how Delphi differs from Delbecq.
5. List and describe several of the most commonly used statistics.

RESOURCE

GOAL PRIORITIES: A CONSENSUS-SEEKING ACTIVITY*

Goals

  I. To assist the group to assess its values.

 II. To focus on the group decision-making process.

III. To discover evolving leadership in the group.

* Source: Michael E. O'Neill and Kai R. Martensen, *Criminal Justice Group Training: A Facilitators Handbook,* La Jolla, CA.,: University Associates, 1975, pp. 44-48.

Group Size
A minimum of three groups and a maximum of five groups, each composed of three to five participants.

Time Required
Approximately one and one-half hours.

Materials
  I. A copy of the summary of the reports of the National Advisory Commission on Criminal Justice Standards and Goals for each participant. (See Appendix A.)
  II. A copy of the Goal Priorities Assessment Sheet for each participant.
  III. A copy of the Goal Priorities Observer Form for each observer.
  IV. Newsprint and a felt-tipped marker.
  V. Pencils for all participants.

Physical Setting
A large room with adjacent areas for small groups to meet.

Process
  I. The facilitator distributes to each participant a copy of the standards and goals compiled by the National Advisory Commission on Criminal Justice Standards and Goals. He gives a brief overview of the report.
  II. The facilitator then distributes the Goal Priorities Assessment Sheet and has each participant establish priorities for the goals. (Fifteen minutes.)
  III. The participants then form small subgroups to establish priorities for the goals based on group concensus. One member of each subgroup may be the process observer; he receives a copy of the Goal Priorities Observer Form. (Thirty minutes.)

Notes on the Use of "Goal Priorities":

GOAL PRIORITIES ASSESSMENT SHEET

Instructions: Rank the following police goals in order of importance. Place a "1" in front of the most important, a "7" in front of the least important.

Ranking (Priority)

Individual	Group	Goal
_____	_____	To develop fully the potential fo the criminal justice system to apprehend offenders.
_____	_____	To establish teamwork between police and citizens.
_____	_____	To establish teamwork among members of the criminal justice system.
_____	_____	To clearly determine an act on the local crime problem.
_____	_____	To make the most of human resources.
_____	_____	To make the most of technological resources.
_____	_____	To develop fully the police response to special community needs.

GOAL PRIORITIES OBSERVER FORM

1. What value differences were identifiable within the group?

2. How were the differences resolved?

3. Who readily accepted the consensus on priorities? Who did not?

4. How were decisions reached by the group?

5. What *facilitating* leadership behaviors emerged in the discussion?

6. What *inhibiting* leadership behaviors were observed?

IV. The facilitator asks each subgroup to reveal its goal priorities; these are listed on newsprint by the facilitator.

V. The total group discusses members' agreements and disagreements with the listed priorities.

Variations

See Pfeiffer and Jones, Volume IV, p. 54.

Sources

Jones, J.E. Synergy and concensus-seeking. In J.E. Jones & J.W. Pfeiffer (Eds.), *The 1973 annual handbook for group facilitators*. La Jolla, Ca.: University Associates, 1973.

Structured Experiences 11, 15, 30, 64, 69, and 115. In J.W. Pfeiffer & J.E. Jones (Eds.), *A handbook of structured experiences for human relations training* (Vols. I, II, III, and IV). La Jolla, Ca.: University Associates, 1969 & 1974; 1970 & 1974; 1971 & 1974; 1973.

Structured Experience 77. In J.W. Pfeiffer & J.E. Jones (Eds.), *The 1972 annual handbook for group facilitators*, La Jolla, Ca.: University Associates, 1972.

REFERENCES

Anderson, Theodore and Morris Zeldatch, *A Basic Course in Statistics: With Sociological Implications*, 2nd ed., New York: Holt, Rinehart and Winston, Inc., 1968. A step by step guide for computing and using basic statistics. Provides specific examples of each statistical technique.

A study conducted for the Illinois Law Enforcement Commission, *Evaluation of the Illinois Crime Laboratory System*, unpublished report, January, 1975. Reviews all aspects of the state of Illinois crime laboratory systems. Points out limitations and provides specific recommendations for improvement of the system.

Dalker, Norman C., *Delphi*, Santa Monica, California: The Rand Corporation, 1968. An in-depth evaluation of the application of techniques and Delphi to long range planning.

Delbecq, Andrew and Andrew Vande Ven, "A Group Process Model for Problem Identification and Program Planning," *Journal of Applied Behavioral Sciences*, Vol. 7, July-August 1971, pp. 466-492. Emphasizes the use of group processes to planning and identification of organizational problems.

Edwards, Allen, *Statistical Methods*, 2nd ed., New York: Holt, Rinehart and Winston, Inc., 1967. A text designed for individuals who have a limited amount of mathematical background.

Etzel, Michael, et al, "A Modified Nominal-Group Process for Public Sector Problem Solving," *Public Personnel Management Journal*, September-October, 1974, pp. 439-446. Critiques the use of some techniques for group problem solving. Suggests a modified group has more merit.

Gordon, T. J. and Olaf Helmer, *Report on a Long Range Forecasting Study*, Santa Monica, California: Rand Corporation, 1964. Takes a comprehensive look at applying techniques and Delphi to long range planning.

Kraemer, Kenneth, *Policy Analysis in Local Government*, Washington, D.C.: International City Management Association, 1973. This text gives an in-depth practical discussion on the use of models in the government setting. Models relative to inventory theory, queuing theory, simulations, operational gaming, and senarios are discussed in terms of their use in the government setting.

Larsons, R.C., *Urban Police Patrol Analysis*, Boston: MIT Press, 1972. Discusses applicability and use of queing to aid in the allocation of police patrol units.

National Advisory Commission on Criminal Justice Standards and Goals, *Criminal Justice System*, Washington, D.C.: U. S. Government Printing Office, 1973, p. 238. Provides a complete systems approach to analyzing the criminal justice agencies.

Newman, Robert and Aberstone Jollee, *Evaluation Technology*, A report prepared for the Los Angeles Regional Criminal Justice Planning Board, January 1972. Discusses applicable evaluation strategies as applied to criminal justice.

O'Neill, Michael and Kai Martensen, *Criminal Justice Group Training–A Facilitated Handbook*, La Jolla, California: University Associates, 1975. Provides a complete reference and use of structured experiences in criminal justice.

Team Policing–Seven Case Studies, Washington, D. C.: Police Foundation, 1973. Presents seven documented case studies on team policing in seven cities.

Unsinger, Dr. Peter, discussion paper of PERT prepared for San Jose State University Police Middle Management Programs, unpublished, 1974. Describes the steps and use of PERT for criminal justice use.

Unwin, Dr. Ernest, Consultant, A Seminar Training Paper, unpublished, 1975. Presents an overview of modeling uses in criminal justice.

Chapter Objectives

1. Provide a means for the systematic identification of problem solving solutions.
2. Illustrate techniques for the development of solution oriented projects.
3. The concept of the planner as a salesman is discussed.
4. Develop a methodology for the systematic selection of solutions for implementation.
5. Emphasize the importance of implementing solutions which directly impact problems.
6. Illustrate the importance of integrating solutions with each of the components of the criminal justice system.
7. Illustrate the use of the matrix as an organization and planning tool.
8. The format for a project description is illustrated and its use in the solution selection process is displayed.

5

Identifying and Selecting Feasible Alternative Problem Solutions

The objective of this step in the planning process is to systematically identify and select alternative problem solving solutions. These solutions will be developed in direct response to the presented goals and objectives that were described in the previous chapters and which were set by the policy makers of the planning organization. Hence the solutions contribute toward the solving of the priority problems facing the criminal justice system. After solutions are identified, it then becomes necessary to select the solution or solutions that will best satisfy the prestated problems, goals, objective resources and constraints. The identification and selection of solutions is a difficult task and the planning process provides the least assistance. However, there are approaches and planning tools which can help organize one's thinking, searching and selection.

Determination of Criminal Justice System Involvement

The first point in the development of alternative solutions is to examine the functions of each element of the criminal justice system and determine if, in any way, they can contribute significantly to the accomplishment of a given objective, goal or program. The purpose of this effort is to encourage the consideration of all resources available to the criminal justice system, and the cooperation and coordination of the system components involved.

During this step the initiative for the planning effort passes, in most cases, to the operating agencies within the system. This insures that those who will be responsible for implementing solutions help to determine what that solution will be. The planning staff and their policy advisors should, however, continue to provide direction and guidance by first identifying the components of the criminal justice system who may be involved in attaining a stated objective, then by establishing criteria for this selection among the alternatives and finally by making available the resources for implementation for those alternatives that meet the selection criteria.

In Chapter I we discussed the roles, responsibilities and functions of each of the criminal justice system agecies. Below is a summary of those functions that will prove useful as we attempt to relate the responsibility for the identification of alternative solutions by agency.

The breakdown of functions can vary, depending upon the level of planning and analysis. For example, if planning is being done for one agency within the system, the above listed

Criminal Justice System Component	Functions
Law Enforcement	
a. Police, Sheriff, Private patrols, Special district police.	Deterence.
Courts	
a. District Attorney	Prosecution.
b. Public Defender	Defense.
c. Justice/Municipal/ Superior Courts	Guilt Determination/Sentencing.
d. Defense Attorney	Defense.
Corrections	
a. Probation	Non Institutional Rehabilitation.
b. Corrections	Institutional Rehabilitation.

Community Based

a. Education Agencies — Crime Prevention. Crisis Intervention. Court Referral. Post Release. Service.

b. Health Agencies, Welfare Agencies Community Based Agencies — Social Service.

system components might be the various departments or divisions within a given agency. The functions, then, would describe the responsibility/capability of each department.

One method for identifying the system components most likely to be involved in solving a particular problem through the accomplishment of specific goals and objectives is seen in Figure V-1.

In this example the problems, goals and objectives are listed in priority order in the horizontal plane while the system components are listed in the vertical plane thus forming a

Problems / System Component	#1 PRIORITY PROBLEM				#2 PRIORITY PROBLEM			
	#1 Priority Goal		#2 Priority Goal		#1 Priority Goal		#2 Priority Goal	
	#1 Obj.	#2 Obj.	#1 Obj.	#2 Obj.	#1 Obj.	#2 Obj.	#1 Obj.	#2 Obj.
Law Enforcement								
a. Police	X				X	X		
b. Sheriff		X	X					
c. Private								
Courts								
a. D.A.	X	X		X	X	X	X	
b. Public Defender								

FIGURE V-1. System Component Involvement Matrix.

matrix. Obviously there may be more than 2 problems or 2 goals and/or 2 objectives for each goal. Build the matrix to fit the results of your particular problem identification and goal and objective setting process. Next mark the boxes of the matrix indicating which system component can contribute to the accomplishment of a stated objective. You may also want to note briefly in each box what resource each component can provide.

To further illustrate this matrix, let us assume that our planning organization identified the below stated situation:

Problem: Dangerous drug and narcotic usage by juveniles is increasing at an alarming rate.

Goal: Reduce the use of dangerous drugs and narcotics by juveniles.

Objective: Reduce juvenile dangerous drugs and narcotics usage by 30% in 36 months.

Solution Project
Under Consideration: Develop and conduct one country-wide educational program for youth on the hazards of narcotics and dangerous drug usage over a 12 month period.

Solution Project
Expectation: Reduce the use of dangerous drugs and narcotics by juveniles 10% in 36 months. The matrix for this situation might then be as depicted in Figure V-2.

In this example, the planners have indicated the primary manner in which each type of agency will most likely be involved (i.e., personnel and training, facilities and equipment, other) and the type of agency which should be responsible for coordinating planning efforts related to this objective. The method for determining the involvement of various organizations may be accomplished in a variety of ways but will generally depend on several considerations, including:

- Knowledge of causes underlying the problem, as demonstrated by previous studies and experience.
- Knowledge of the capabilities of the types of agencies involved.

PROBLEM GOAL, OBJECTIVE, SOLUTION, PROJECT EXPECT. ⟋ SYSTEM COMPONENT	#1 PROBLEM JUVENILE USEAGE OF DRUGS AND NARCOTICS	
	#1 GOAL — Reduce Juvenile Drug and Narcotic Useage	
	#1 OBJECTIVE — Reduce Juvenile Drug and Narcotic Useage 30% in 36 months	
	SOLUTION/PROJECT A Develop & Conduct 1 County-wide Education Program in 12 Months	SOLUTION/PROJECT B Establish 3 Neighborhood Walk in Centers in 36 Months
	SOLUTION/PROJECT Expectation Reduce Juvenile Drug and Narcotic Useage 10% in 36 Months	SOLUTION/PROJECT Expectation Reduce Juvenile Drug and Narcotic Useage 10% in 36 Months
Law Enforcement		
a. Police	X Personnel & Training	
b. Sheriff	X Personnel & Training	
c. Other		
Courts		
a. D.A.		
b. Public Defender		
c. Courts		
d. Defense Attorney		
Corrections		
a. Probation	X Personnel & Training Develop Training for Other Agencies	
b. Corrections	X Personnel & Training Facilities & Equipment	
Community		
a. Education Agencies	X Personnel & Training Facilities & Equipment Primary Youth Contact	
b. Health Agencies	X Personnel & Training Expertise on Drug Effects	

FIGURE V-2. System Component Involvement Matrix.

- Relationship of the planning organization to the organizational components in terms of authority.

If this stage of the planning process is being conducted within a given system component agency rather than across multi-component boundaries, the component column of the matrix just illustrated would contain the various departments, sections or people within that component. The same analysis process would exist in relating the various departments to each of the problems, goals and objectives.

Solution Development

At this point the planner must get out of his ivory tower and down to his most persuasive and salesmanship-oriented personality. Each agency that has contributed to the achievement of an objective and that has been identified by the foregoing matrix must be contacted and sold on the idea of developing a solution. This task becomes progressively easier for the planner if he has involved Criminal Justice people in problem solving, goal determination, objective, identification, and formulation efforts. The salesmanship job is also easier when the planner can offer resource assistance, for example grant funds and staff assistance in the development of projects. One word of caution, however, too much planning staff involvement in the development of agency projects results in a loss of commitment within that agency to assure that the project will be a success. They will loose sight of being part of the project and feel it is being imposed from the outside.

Once you have the commitment of the system component to participate in and formulate a project to achieve an objective, how do you go about thinking of a project to implement?

At this point we are looking for a word or phrase that tends to suggest solution oriented project concept. We are not looking for a complete and detailed project description. For many crimes the solution is quite evident. As in the juvenile drug education objective stated earlier, it is quite clear that what is called for is the establishment of an education project and the delivering of specific juvenile education.

Many times solution oriented projects can be borrowed from other agencies who have similar problems and have already implemented one or more solutions. One of the best resources for obtaining examples of projects that have been implemented elsewhere is the regional planning unit (RPU) of your state planning agency. (SPA). This source can provide examples of projects which have operated in a given state and perhaps of projects within this specific region or county. Another source of information is through the National Institute of Law Enforcement and Criminal Justice (NILECJ) who, under the Law Enforcement Assistance Administration (LEAA), provides a national reference service of LEAA funded projects and other publications concerning the criminal justice system. In addition to these sources of project suggestions consideration may be given to some of the state and national professional trade journals associated with Criminal Justice Agencies. They typically feature successful projects.

If all else fails, "brainstorming" may be required. A conference is called of all those working on a problem. They meet to think up ideas for its solution. All criticism is barred. Quantity of suggestions rather than quality is the aim. The last two sentences prevent fruitful ideas from being stillborn, either by group censure or by self censure. A great many ideas produced in such a session may be foolish and infeasible, for example, legalize crime. It is better to have twenty foolish ideas and ten good ones in a total of thirty, than two foolish ones and three good ones in a total of five. Subsequent criticism can easily eliminate the foolishness, for competent criticism is easier to obtain than competent creativity.

The total output of such a group, where one person's idea may suggest something further to another individual, has been found more often than not to be greater than the total of ideas advanced by the same number of people working in isolation.

When a list of ideas is produced, more ideas can usually be generated by taking combinations of those on the list. The potential is greater than merely the combination of all the pairs on the list. As illustrated by Arthur D. Hall (Hall, 1968, p. 456) "the potential number of ideas that can be obtained from "n" ideas is:

$$c_2^n + c_3^n + c_4^n + \cdots c_n^a, \text{ where } c_r^n = n \ !/(n\text{-}r) \ ! \ r \ !$$

where C is a combination derived from n idea and r is the total number of ideas considered."

In addition to just generating ideas, brainstorming can be used to create new solution-oriented concepts rather than relying on many womewhat overplayed and over implemented solutions which have been, in the past, only partially successful.

At this point, many theoretical planners would challenge the foregoing concept of allowing the involved system component to generate their own solution or project ideas. The alternative, of course, would be for the planner to define a grand program to solve a problem. Then he would simply require each component to implement their portion of the program under his direction. Unfortunately, in most cases the advanced status of the art in criminal justice planning is not there yet. Planners are not fully recognized as being an asset beyond a potential source for grant funds or a resource for the accomplishment of special non-related research activities. This is further complicated by the process nature of the non-system criminal justice system that was discussed in Chapter 1. No one person or body of people including planners have authority to demand change from the criminal justice system. At best, the planner through salesmanship must sell his recommendations to the system components and coordinate their efforts in implementing these changes. The result is that the shortest distance between two points is not necessarily a straight line and the planner becomes an expert in the art of compromise.

Selecting The Best Solution

As we get into solution or project selection a further comment becomes appropriate. The process we just completed (determining criminal justice system involvement and encouraging system components to develop solutions) may not be appropriate n some planning situations. Many times the Criminal Justice planner is faced with a multitude of project solutions from all or a few of the criminal justice system agencies. It then becomes his job to recommend the best solution for implementation. However, the planner must be cautious not to put all his eggs in one basket, that is, he should seek a balance of solutions for implementation from each of the system components. Local pressure and politics will usually seek an over abundance of police and community based oriented projects. Outside funding pressures, however, will be trying to encourage court and corrections projects. A mix between the two becomes the tightrope which the planner should seek to walk.

Descriptive Preparation

Each of the solutions that were generated as project concepts or titles by the solution development effort must now be described in greater detail before the solution selection process can continue. The general format of this expanded description should include the following information:

- Title of Project—The title should be descriptive but limited to one or two lines.
- Project Expectations—The expectations should describe the measurable results which the improvement is meant to accomplish; the expectations should be, in effect, a restatement, clarification, quantification, and further definition of the related problem goal and objective statement.
- Major Tasks to be accomplished—The general steps, or tasks, to be implemented to accomplish the above stated expectations should be described in detail sufficient to allow those responsible for selecting among alternatives to understand what is planned.
- Responsibilities—Organizational responsibility for the task activities should be clearly described. This may simply be the implementing agency or department to include the project director.
- Resources—The resources (i.e., personnel, equipment, facilities) required must be identified; the availability of critical resources (i.e., key individuals, one-of-a-kind facilities) should be determined.

- Budgets—Both the implementation and operational costs should be estimated; the estimates must distinguish between out-of-pocket costs and the prorated costs of existing resources. Typical budget expense categories used are:
  - personal services
  - supplies and operations
  - travel/conferences
  - consultant services/construction
  - equipment
- Schedules—The elapsed time required to complete each task activities should be estimated. Measure from the date implementation is started.
- Risk—Estimate potential risk which could result due to project failure. Intuitively estimate a percent figure of potential failure for each risk area identified.

The magnitude of this expanded description should be three to five pages in length. An example of a project summary using this format is illustrated in the Resource section of this chapter.

This request for expanded solution description is sometimes viewed by local agencies as the first step of the bureaucratic process and may bring complaints about the paper work. It is better to spend time in drafting 3 to 5 papers prior to project activation than it would be to implement a project for thousands of dollars and ultimately find out it is not solving a problem.

Solution/Problem Analysis

As expanded solution descriptions are received from the components of the system the first step in the selection analysis process is to identify those solutions that best address the highest priority stated problems, goals and objectives set forth by the policy people directing the planning organization. If the criminal justice system involvement activity has been used, this analysis will serve as a cross check to assure that the solutions which have been submitted still conform to the goals and objectives that the planning organization seeks to accomplish.

If solutions are solicited in a blanket fashion from all agencies, this analysis will be useful in doing a first sort in order to determine which of the proposed solutions are related to the accomplishments of the stated goals and objectives.

A tool useful in performing this analysis is shown in Figure V-3.

As the Project expectation portion of the solution is read, the immediately foregoing matrix simply indicates which priority problem goal and objective is being addressed. The matrix will display those solutions which will implement the highest priority objectives and goals, thus solving the highest priority problems. From this example it can be seen that solutions A, B and C are preferable to solutions D and E. The first solutions are attempting to solve the number one priority problem; therefor, from this analysis, solutions D and E could be eliminated. The cut-off point is subjective and can extend beyond the first problem if resources permit.

Resource/Feasibility

The next step of the project selection process consists of further expansion of the project descriptions that are most related to

Problem / Solution	#1 PRIORITY PROBLEM				#2 PRIORITY PROBLEM			
	#1 Priority Goal		#2 Priority Goal		#1 Priority Goal		#2 Priority Goal	
	#1 Obj.	#2 Obj.	#1 Obj.	#2 Obj.	#1 Obj.	#2 Obj.	#1 Obj.	#2 Obj.
SOLUTION/PROJECT #A	X			X				
SOLUTION/PROJECT #B	X	X	X					
SOLUTION/PROJECT #C	X	X	X	X				
SOLUTION/PROJECT #D					X		X	X
SOLUTION/PROJECT #E	X					X		

FIGURE V-3. Problem/Solution Analysis Matrix.

identifying and selecting feasible alternative problem solutions   **123** the high priority problem, goal and objective areas in order to determine their resource needs and their potential feasibility for success.

As stated in "A Criminal Justice Planning Guide" (California Council on Criminal Justice, 1972, p. 2-39):

> The criteria to be used in selecting among alternative improvements should be established by the policy makers of the planning organization and communicated to the organzational components involved. These criteria provide additional direction and guidance, improving the chances of acceptable and workable improvements being developed.

The selection criteria are commonly grouped into two major categories. The first are resource requirements. Typical requirements are described below:

- Financial—How much money is required to accomplish the solution? Which solution requires the least money?
- Manpower—What are the manpower requirements needed to implement and operate the solution? Which project will use the least manpower? What is the dollar cost of the manpower needs?
- Equipment—Are there special equipment needs that must be acquired to implement the solution? Which alternative requires the acquisition of the least amount of equipment? How much will the needed equipment cost?
- Facilities—Are facilities available to house the solution operation? Which solution will require the least amount of additional funds? What will the facilities cost?
- Knowledge—Does the system component responsible for the implementation of the solution have the "know-how" necessary to implement and operate the solution? How much will consultant services cost if knowledge is required?
- Time—How long will it take the solution to accomplish its stated objectives? Which solution offers the quickest results?

Using a matrix similar to Figure V-4 analysis can be made of each solution in view of each of the above criteria. Since all of the above criteria are equateable to dollars except for time, which can be measured in months, use can be made of these as a common analysis measure. To complete the resource component, each of the solutions must be reviewed in view of their dollar amounts or time, and place them in descending rank order, seeking minimum amounts, and totaling the values for each solution. The solution with the smallest total would rank highest by this methodology. This technique is illustrated in Figure V-4.

From the above analysis the best solution would be solution C with a rank score of 8. Second and third best solutions would be solutions B and A respectively.

The second major category of selection criteria is Feasibility. These criteria are typical as described below:

- Resource—The feasibility for obtaining the resources described above are considered. Generally, the less resources that are required the easier they are to obtain.
- Political—This takes into consideration the agency and community politics that would influence the implementation and operation of each solution.
- Impact—Which solution will have the greatest impact in solving the prioritized problem, goals and objectives.
- Risk—Which alternative has the least amount of risk or greatest possibility for success in the accomplishment of its stated objective. A feel for the risk factor can be obtained from the project summary if the suggested format is used.

Again, using a matrix we can analyze each solution in view of each of the above feasibility criteria. Unfortunately this time we have no convenient means of quantifying the analysis measures. Therefore, we must rank each criteria subjectively using our own best judgment. That is, in analyzing political feasibility between the solution alternatives, simply ask yourself which of the alternatives is most politically feasible to implement and operate; then rate it with a number 1. Then rate the next most politically feasible and so on, with the remainder of the alternatives and criteria. To complete the feasibility matrix, total the individual ratings for each solution. The solution with the lowest rating is the most feasible according to this

Resource / Solution	FINANCIAL	MANPOWER	EQUIPMENT	FACILITIES	KNOWLEDGE	TIME	TOTAL RANKING
SOLUTION A — $ OR MO.	180,000	103,200	6,000	10,800	30,000	36 MO.	15
SOLUTION A — RANK	3	2	2	3	3	2	
SOLUTION B — $ OR MO.	135,000	103,800	4,000	7,200	20,000	24 MO.	11
SOLUTION B — RANK	2	3	1	2	2	1	
SOLUTION C — $ OR MO.	36,000	32,000	4,000	0	0	48 MO.	8
SOLUTION C — RANK	1	1	1	1	1	3	

FIGURE V-4. Resource Analysis Matrix.

analysis technique. The use of the feasibility analysis matrix is illustrated in Figure V-5.

From the above matrix the most feasible solution is A with a rank score of 7. Second and third best would be solutions C and B respectively.

Summary Analysis

In order to complete the solution analysis and arrive at a solution oriented project recommendation, the information we gathered from the solution/problem analysis matrix, the resource analysis matrix and the feasibility analysis must be brought together and viewed in totality. The relative importance of the results from the foregoing matrix analysis should be indicated. The purpose is to produce a numerical indicator, or weight, that conveys the combined judgment of those responsible for selecting among the alternative solutions. Generally, the weight assigned to the matrix analysis data will be subjective and meaningful only in relation to other criteria and for that situation.

In the example shown below in Figure V-6 the solution/problem analysis matrix data is approximately six times as important as the feasibility analysis data. Because of the nature of the resource analysis data it is three times as important as feasibility data, and only half as important as the solution/problem data.

Feasibility / Solution	RESOURCE	POLITICAL	IMPACT	RISK	TOTAL RANKING
SOLUTION A	3	2	1	1	7
SOLUTION B	2	3	2	2	9
SOLUTION C	1	1	3	3	8

FIGURE V-5. Feasibility Analysis Matrix.

As an illustration, three matrix analysis data components have been scored in Figure V-6. For each selection criterion, a raw score of one (1) was assigned to the most desirable alternative; a raw score of two (2) was assigned to the second most desirable alternative; and a raw score of three (3) was assigned to the least desirable alternative. This assignment of raw scores was based on the combined judgment of those responsible for selecting among alternatives. Once the raw scores have been assigned, the weighted scores are determined. Based on the total weighted scores in the example, Solution C is preferred, followed by Solution B and, finally, Solution A.

The final selection of the solution alternative is generally performed by the policy makers of the planning organization in view of the foregoing matrix analysis. Throughout this suggested project selection process it is not the use of the various matrixes that is important, rather it is the logical thought process that is employed. First, the assurance that the pro-

Solution / Matrix Analysis Data	WEIGHT FACTOR	SOLUTION A	SOLUTION B	SOLUTION C
SOLUTION PROBLEM ANALYSIS	0.6X	3=1.8	2=1.2	1=0.6
RESOURCE ANALYSIS	0.3X	3=0.9	2=0.6	1=0.3
FEASIBILITY ANALYSIS	0.1X	2=0.2	1=0.1	3=0.3
TOTAL	1.0	2.9	1.9	1.2

FIGURE V-6. Summary Analysis Matrix.

posed alternatives treat the high priority problem areas. Second, that the project solutions proposed are within the resources available, i.e., money, manpower, equipment, facilities, knowledge and time. Lastly, that the project alternatives are within the realm of feasibility. Now the planners role in the selection process is finished.

System Impact

With the selection of the preferred alternatives, the planning organization has defined how it intends to go about solving the major problems it faces. By the conclusion of this step the major elements of the comprehensive criminal justice plan may have been completed. However, further planning is required in order to assure that those projects to be implemented do not create more problems than they cure elsewhere in the system.

Without the use of overly sophisticated and complex criminal justice system computer models, it is almost impossible to predict accurately the impact of any crime reducing activity or criminal justice system improvement planning. However, a quick and simple method is available for projects designed to impact arrests or diversions from the system. This method can be employed with data typically available from state crime statistics offices.

As an example, let's assume that the Sheriff's Office of Monterey County, California, a medium size county, wants to implement a county narcotics bureau whose objective is to increase felony drug arrests of non-user/sellers by 150 during the upcoming year. If one uses a criminal justice system flow chart as illustrated in Figure V-7 and fill in each box with the most recent full calendar year arrest and disposition base data available one can project quantity and percent changes for each of the boxes shown.

In the base year there were 2915 felony arrests. Five percent were released, 2.5% were transferred to other jurisdictions, 91% resulted in felony complaints and 1.5% were filed as misdemeanors. If the new County narcotics bureau had been implemented in the base year and if it accomplished its objective of 150 felony arrests, then the felony arrest figure would

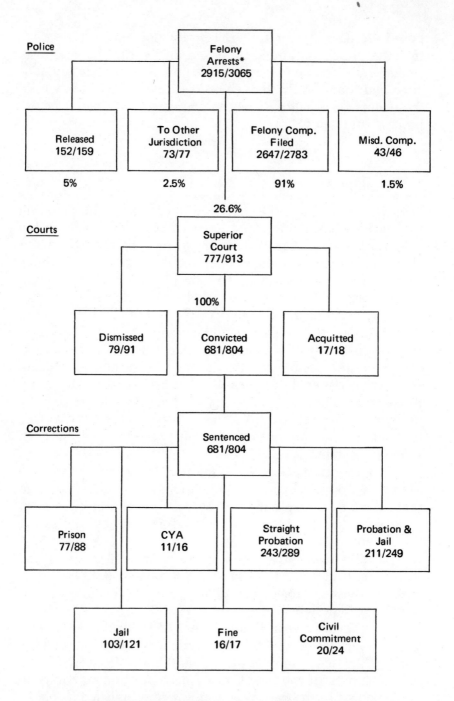

FIGURE V-7. Criminal Justice System Flow Chart.

have been 3065. This means that instead of 152 people being released, 159 would have been released if we assume the 5% of total arrests remains constant. If this same analysis is carried out for the remainder of the boxes in the flow chart the planner can get a feel for the quantity and percent change impact that a project may have. The next step then is for the planner to contact each element in the system and forewarn them of the potential change. For example, the District Attorney might be contacted and asked if he can handle another 139 felony complaints filed per year with his present staff. His answer may be that he will need to add another investigator or trial lawyer.

Similar responses may be received from the courts and corrections areas when they learn of their expected workload increase. This is planning ahead.

Remember, however, this is a quick and simple analysis method. It's using old data that does not consider current year felony arrest increases or decreases. It assumes that the percent relationship will remain constant and it assumes the project will achieve its objective. It does not consider the reality that most of the project arrests will take place during the latter part of the project's first year due to start up activities in the early part of the project's first year. Even with all these threatening cautions, experience has indicated that this type of analysis can be within 95%-98% accurate in its predictions on a year-to-year basis using one year old base data. Obviously the accuracy may change if the analysis is employed in high urban or small rural areas because of the simple impact of crime volumes on percentages over a very large or very small service population.

The same approach can be used on diversion projects. In this instance the impact will be more on the sentencing agencies or courts depending upon where the diversion process takes place. If a new flow chart is developed for juvenile justice system projects, increasing arrests of juveniles or increasing juvenile diversion from the system can be assessed for system impact.

Summary

In this chapter, goal and objective statements that should be utilized by criminal justice agencies have been identified.

Through various techniques such as secondary research, salesmanship and brainstorming, planners can encourage these involved agencies to develop solution oriented projects. The format for the further description of the solution alternatives identified is described and illustrated. From information learned from problem/solution, resource, feasibility and summary analysis matrix techniques, the planner and his policy making participants can select the best solution for implementation. It must be kept in mind, there is nothing magic about using the matrix as an analysis process, rather it is the logical and systematic thinking that goes into filling in the matrix that forces the user to consider each criteria equally in view of each alternative being considered. Even the criteria suggested in this chapter for each of the matrices need not be the only criteria to be considered. It is illustrative of the types of factors that should be considered. Analytically the selected solution has been tested for its probable impact on the other elements of the criminal justice system; and the agencies have been made aware so they can take this into consideration in their planning. Now project implementation may begin, through the process of planning, as illustrated in Chapter VI.

Topics for Discussion

1. Discuss the importance of having each element of the criminal justice system participate in problem solving.
2. One of the best methods of identifying solution alternatives is to see what other agencies with similar problems have implemented as projects. Identify the hazards of relying solely on this method as a source for generating solutions.
3. Discuss the matrix technique in the selection of the best solution.
4. Discuss the criminal justice planner as a salesman.
5. Distinguish between the responsibilities of the planner and the policy maker during the project selection process.
6. Discuss the importance of assessing the impact of a given solution before it is implemented.
7. Discuss the simple system impact evaluation technique.

RESOURCE

PROJECT SUMMARY*

1. TITLE: Burglary Crime Prevention
2. *Project Expectations:*
   a. Reduce reported burglaries reported 15% less than the 1975 reported rate per hundred thousand in 36 months.
   b. Increase burglary arrests by 10% over the 1975 arrest rate per hundred thousand in 36 months.
   c. Increase the burglary clearance rate by 10% over the 1975 clearance rate per hundred thousand in 36 months.
   d. Increase the value of stolen property recovered by 25% over the 1975 value in 36 months.

3. *Major Tasks To Be Accomplished:*

   Task A—Target Hardening

   Through the use of paid senior citizens contact each private residence, and concerned business in the city and perform facility security check. Mark and identify valuable property, and distribute burglary prevention literature.

   Task B—Improved Caseload Management

   After the completion of a case by case load study determine which cases have the greatest potential for being solved in priority of the available evidence and other relevant factors. Assign detective resources based upon these determined case priorities.

   Task C—Improved Crime Data Analysis

   Based upon past burglary statistics develop a predictive crime incidence model and allocate patrol and target hardening resources on a continual basis to the areas of the city exhibiting

---

* A typical project summary which presents a burglary prevention project.

the greatest potential for burglaries as predicted by the model and officer experience.

4. *Responsibilities:*
>   City of _____ Police Department,
>   Chief of Police _____ Project Director.

5. *Resources:*

Task A

Community senior citizen clubs, Police aids, student summer hirees, vibrator marking tools, crime prevention literature and premises security check training.

Task B

Consultant study services, detective training.

Task C

Consultant study services, limited off time computer services and patrol training.

6. *Budgets:*

Expenditure	Task A	Task B	Task C	Total
Personal Services	$20,000	$ 2,000	$ 2,000	$24,000
Consultant Services		10,000	10,000	20,000
Travel/Conferences	5,000			5,000
Supplies & Operation	5,000		5,000	10,000
Equipment	500			500
TOTAL	$30,000	$12,000	$17,000	$59,000

7. *Risk*
Task A

The result will probably be an increase in crimes reported initially. Also some difficulty might be experienced in getting the paid volunteers organized. 5% risk factor.

Task B

The major risk will be in convincing the detectives to follow the case investigation guidelines and priorities defined from the study. 5% risk factor.

Task C

The primary risk will be in the quality of historical data and in the assurance that the patrol division allocates its forces according to the crime predictions. 10% risk factor.

This project has an 80% potential for success or a 20% chance of failure.

REFERENCES

A Guide for Criminal Justice Planning, a booklet produced by the California Council on Criminal Justice, unpublished, 1971, 67 pgs. A guide used by the California State Planning Agency and Regional Planning Units for the preparation of their 1971 comprehensive criminal justice system plans.

Connor, Patrick E., *Dimensions in Modern Management,* Boston: Houghton Mifflin Co., 1974. A management reader text. Part two has eight selected articles on general management planning.

Hall, Arthur D., *A Methodology for Systems Engineering,* New Jersey: D. Van Nostrand Company, Inc., 1962, p. 456. The subject of this book is the methodology or process of systems engineering, with its contents of tools, case histories and history of the field.

Howlett, Fred and Hunter Hurst, "A Systems Approach to Comprehensive Criminal Justice Planning," *Crime and Delinquency,* Vol. 18, No. 4, October 1971. Discusses the organizational impact of criminal justice planning on the total system.

Lynch, Ronald, *The Police Manager,* Boston: Holbrook Press, 1975. A general police management text. Selected chapters cover planning and selection of feasible solutions.

Chapter Objectives

1. Introduces the importance of developing a strategy for the implementation of a given solution.
2. Indicates a procedure under which the stragety can be developed.
3. Stresses the importance of being sure that all parties to the solution are aware of their roles, responsibilities and expectations.
4. Illustrates the life cycle of a project as it passes through time.
5. Describes and defines the elements of and the need for a work plan.
6. Discusses how the projects activities should be defined by tasks.
7. Relates the budgeting techniques of the projects resources and how they should coincide to the project tasks.
8. Illustrates the task structure as a means of developing schedules.
9. Indicates how the projects life cycle is tied together by the evaluation plan feedback loop.

6
Implementation Planning

Once the decision has been made to proceed with a preferred solution alternative, a more detailed plan for implementation must be developed. Implementation is the process of turning plans into action. Hence, the plan for implementation should provide for the development of:

- An Implementation Strategy
- A Work Plan and
- A Reporting and Evaluation Plan

The plan for implementation should provide the coordination, control and evaluation of the planned activities. The success of planning is largely determined by the success of these implemented improvements. The relationship of the requirements of implementation planning to the preceding steps is discussed below.

Implementation Strategy

The initial task in preparing for implementation is the statement of the strategy to be employed in the implementation of the solution alternative. Strategy defines the framework for effecting the plan. The project summary developed as part of the selection process can now be used as the framework for building this implementation plan and for presenting questions that need to be answered as part of the implementation strategy. The areas to be described in terms of strategy include:

- Agreement of project expectations.
- Organizational responsibilities and relationships.
- General deployment of resources.
- Operational constraints.
- Potential problems.

In many cases these elements will have been developed in earlier steps. However, the information developed previously should be reviewed and restated as necessary to develop a clear, consistent statement of implementation strategy. Only by this means can the commitment and expectations of the parties involved in the implementation of the solution be affirmed.

Agreement of Objectives

All parties to the implementation process need to sit down in a workshop environment and review the project's expectations and tasks as described in the expanded solution description. The individuals involved should include the project director,* the policy people to whom the director reports, and the people responsible for providing the project's resources.

The purpose of the workshop is for the project director to describe and interpret his understanding of each expectation and the tasks necessary to accomplish this expectation in detail to the rest of the participants. All parties involved should reach a "meeting of the minds" such that all are equally communicating and understanding exactly what is involved and expected from the project. Also, and equally important, each project participant should know exactly what is expected from him.

The format of this workshop session should be one of presentation by the project director, and discussion and compromise solutions by the participants. If manpower or financing are not available to accomplish the stated tasks, now is the time to discover it and alter the task, objective and/or project as required to fit the resources actually available. If conflicts arise between the project director, the policy maker and the resource provider, now is the time to get them resolved or may they forever hold their peace.

---

* The title "project director" is used in this chapter to describe the person responsible for the day-to-day operation and management of the project.

Organizational Responsibilities and Relationships

After the expectations and tasks are settled upon, the project director must delineate his organizational responsibilities and relationships with the policy makers and resource providers. The responsibilities and authority the project director can exercise with respect to resources should be carefully delineated, and the authority the project director can exercise in terms of day-to-day operational decisions or project changes must be clarified.

The responsibilities of the resource providers have to be understood and commitments made in order to insure completion of the project. The format for these discussions should be one of the project director stimulation followed by policy maker and resource provider discussion, compromise and conclusion. The output should be a clearly understood set of guidelines indicating the roles, responsibilities and authorities of all project participants.

General Deployment of Resources

As the discussion of responsibilities and relationships is defined, the resource providers need to know when and where their resources will be required. The discussion of resource deployment will permit the project director and resource providers the opportunity to coordinate their activities and needs. The policy makers on the other hand, are present to resolve any conflicts.

Techniques for deploying resources should be discussed and alternatives considered. The project director should be challenged on his recommendations. Generally, the project director becomes so immersed in the carrying out of the project that he loses sight of the fact that it may be a very small portion of the total activities in which the implementing agency is involved. Thus priorities for the commitment of limited resources must be clearly understood by all parties. A community relations project activity for a police department is "small potatoes" compared to the crime fighting and emergency service responsibilities that the department must provide.

Conversely however, the project director must make the policy makers aware when the project is being prioritized out of business. The project director must play the advocate role for the project and fight for its successful completion within commensorate authority and responsibility. It is most definitely a responsibility to alert the policy makers when resources are insufficient to meet the project's expectations.

Operational Constraints

The policy maker must clearly define the boundaries and rules under which the project can operate. The project director must know exactly what can or cannot be done.

Many of these operational constraints are already documented agency policy and should only be changed if their compliance may hamper project activities. This is especially true of covert apprehension and detection projects as alternative to incarceration projects.

It is the project director's responsibility to become thoroughly familiar with fiscal and equipment constraints imposed by any agency from which the funds are received. The use of grant funds demands that the project director become thoroughly familiar with the fiscal affairs manual which serves as a monetary "bible." The primary failure of projects occurs in the accounting for monies in the prescribed manner. Unfortunately common sense and honesty are not always sufficient. Accountants are inclined to set rules and auditors like to catch people violating the rules.

Potential Problems

If participants can complete the foregoing discussions without identifying problems, they are not getting deep enough into the project activities. As problems arise they should be discussed and potential solutions outlined.

Project director contact with similar projects implemented in other jurisdictions will also be helpful. Their experience and advice can be invaluable and should be actively sought. At this stage of the project's development, forewarning of future problems can lead to early and easy solutions.

As can be seen from the previous discussion on implementation strategy meetings, the project director must do alot of prior preparation before confronting the policy makers and resource providers with strategy type questions. The work plan and evaluation plan described in the remainder of this chapter should be completed before the implementation strategy meeting is attempted. These two plans will provide a focal point for meeting discussions and decisions. After the implementation strategy meeting, the project director will have a "design freeze" and the two plans can be updated.

Work Plan

The first step in the development of a work plan is the appointment of a project director who will have responsibility for organizing and implementing the project. Hall has stated that (Hall, 1968, p.128):

> Sometimes he is called the project coordinator to emphasize one of his main functions. He serves as the center of communication on all matters among all the participants, and he is the point of contact with the persons responsible for the provision of the project resources. He allocates the manpower and budget resources to get the project done.

The actual rank or position of the project director is of little concern but needs to be a person who can turn plans into action. The project director must also possess verbal and written communicative skills as well as a thorough understanding of budgetary and scheduling processes. Equally important, the project director must be a persuader and compromiser who is goal oriented. Seldom having the resources to get a job done, reliance must, rather, be placed on ability to convince those persons who control the resources to expend them for the project.

It cannot be overly emphasized that the selection of a qualified project director does more for the potential success of a project than any other single factor.

Project Life Cycle

To better understand the development of a work plan, a brief description of a project's life cycle is useful. Figure VI-1 illustrates a project life cycle.

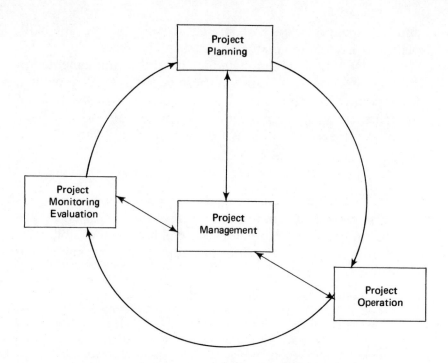

FIGURE VI-1. Project Life Cycle.

Project planning has to do with the preliminary preparation necessary to assure that the project can be implemented. It usually includes work plan development, task development and budget and schedule preparation. Project implementation is simply the actual operation of the project tasks and activities. Project monitoring and evaluation is the policing of the project activities to assure that the tasks and activities are being accomplished as planned. Project management is the function of coordinating the entire project activities to assure that the project is accomplished. It includes the allocation and provision of resources and the day to day decision making to assure smooth project operation.

Work Plan

With this background of the proper selection of a project director and the understanding of a project life cycle, work plan preparation can commence. The purpose of the work plan is to organize the solution alternatives in a manner that will facilitate assignment of responsibility, coordination of effort among resources, and monitoring of costs, schedules and results.

Tasks

The work effort necessary to carry out the planned project should be broken down into manageable, clearly defined work tasks. These tasks provide the basis for developing budgets, milestone schedules and for assigning work responsibilities and resources. The development of tasks begins with the review of the problem, goals, objectives and project expectations (see Figure VI-2). This structure is then expanded down to the level where work assignments can be made to specific organizational elements or individuals. Always two fundamental questions confront the project manager:

- What work activities are necessary to accomplish the project expectations?
- What is the output of this activity?

The number of subdivisions that will be created in the task breakdown structure depends on the size and complexity of the implementation effort and the number of participating organizations or individuals. Responsibility for the completion of task or sub-task is assigned to a specific individual, group, department or agency. In the example shown in Figure VI-2, Project Solution 1 (Develop and conduct one county-wide educational program for youth in (twelve months) consists of six major tasks. One of these major tasks (Develop instructional materials) has been further divided into three distinct sub-tasks. In a larger or more complicated project (i.e. development of a regional justice information system), additional levels of tasks would be required in order to specify work assignments for organizational elements or individuals.

As stated in "A Guide for Criminal Justice Planning" (California Council on Criminal Justice, 1971, p. 2-53):

> A complete description of work tasks does not automatically emerge at the beginning of implementation; it evolves through the life of an improvement as specific tasks are identified. As

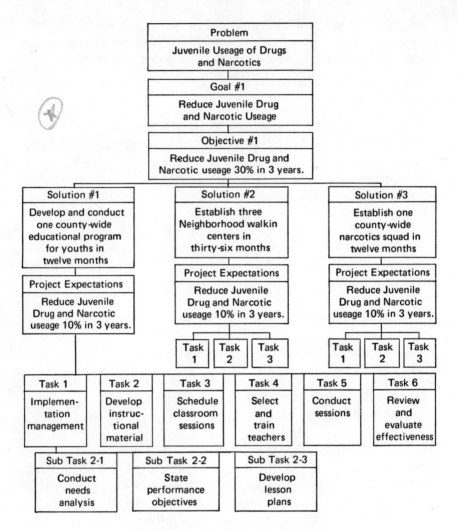

FIGURE VI-2. Task Development.

work proceeds, certain changes to the requirements inevitably develop. Since continuous updating of original plans is an essential part of an effective management control system, procedures must be established to facilitate this process without unduly burdening operating personnel.

Responsibilities for the successful accomplishment of each work task should be assigned to specific organizational elements or individuals. These assignments should be based on the requirements of the tasks and the capabilities of the personnel involved.

Budgets

Each work task must have a budget reflecting the total costs of the activities involved, and an estimation of the time necessary to complete the task. A convenient way for gathering and organizing this information is illustrated in Figure VI-3. The method for gathering this budget data is for the project director to consult with each person or organization responsible for the completion of the task and jointly estimate the costs and time necessary to accomplish the work. The example shown in Figure VI-3 reflects a budget breakdown for the tasks developed in Figure VI-2. The budget breakdown indicated a total project cost of $60,800 (the sum of each of the tasks 1-6). This example includes a consultant who will be paid $30,000 to accomplish sub-tasks 2-1, 2-2 and 2-3. The total project will be completed in 24 weeks, even though the sum of weeks for the individual tasks and sub-tasks is greater than 24 weeks. This is because many of the tasks are occurring at the same time. This is illustrated further in Figure VI-4.

Following are some suggestions for consideration in deriving estimates for each of the different budget categories. The actual location of individual cost items is, of course, dependent upon the rules, regulations and/or guidelines of the resource providing the funding, but the below listed budgeting suggestions are typical of federal grant requirements:

- Personal Service—List each position by title and show the annual salary rate. If the person is employed part-time, list either the hourly rate and number of hours devoted to project (i.e., probation officer, $8 hour for 10 hours = $80); or the yearly salary and percentage of his working time devoted to the project (i.e., probation officer, $12,000/year × 50% = $6000).
- Employee Benefits—Indicate the percentage of the total cost of the benefits allowable to employees assigned to the project. Itemize each benefit by type and percentage (i.e., Public Employees Retirement System 2.8%).
- Travel—Itemize travel expenses of project personnel by purpose and show basis for computation (i.e., conference in San Francisco, 300 miles at .15¢/mile = $45; 2 days per diem @ $25/day = $50).

Budget Category / Work Task	Personal Services $	Consultant Services $	Travel $	Equipment $	Supplies & Operating Expense $	Total $	Time to complete weeks
Task 1 Implementation Management	8,400	—	1,700	750	500	11,350	24 weeks
Task 2 Develop instructional material	—	30,000	—	—	—	30,000	9 weeks
Task 2-1 Conduct needs analysis	—	8,000	—	—	—	8,000	4 weeks
Task 2-2 State performance objectives	—	6,000	—	—	, —	6,000	3 weeks
Task 2-3 Develop Lesson Plan	—	12,000	—	—	—	12,000	6 weeks
Task 3 Schedule classroom	700	—	—	1,500	—	2,200	2 weeks
Task 4 Select and train teachers	2,100	—	450	—	1,300	3,850	6 weeks
Task 5 Conduct Sessions	7,000	—	4,000	—	300	11,300	10 weeks
Task 6 Review & Evaluate	2,100	—	—	—	—	2,100	3 weeks

FIGURE VI-3. Task Budgeting.

- Consultant Services—List each type of consultant and the specific service to be rendered, the proposed fee rates per hour, and the total number of hours devoted to the project.

  For organizations, including professional organizations and educational institutions performing professional services, indicate the type of services being performed and the estimated contract price.
- Equipment—Consider each type of item to be purchased and list separately with unit cost. Rented or leased equipment is typically budgeted as an operating expense. All installation costs included in the purchase of items of equipment are usually budgeted in the Equipment category. The types of items to be considered as equipment are non-expendable major items such as typewriters, desks, etc. Consumable items, i.e. staplers, waste baskets, are usually classified as expendable and are budgeted under supplies and operating expenses.
- Supplies and Operating Expenses—List items within this category by major type (i.e., office supplies, training materials, research forms, equipment maintenance, equipment rental, telephone and postage) and show basis for computation ("x" dollars per month for office supplies, "y" dollars per person for training materials, i.e., unusual supply items, special printing or mailings required for project).

  Actual rent or lease costs are budgeted in this category. Rented or leased equipment can be budgeted as an operating expense.
- Total Project Cost—Itemize the category and task totals and enter in the appropriate box for each row and column.

Milestone Schedules

Schedules define the duration and time sequence of project and task activities. Milestones identify major achievement points in the task activity. Typically this is the expected product output completion date for a given task. Each work task must have a discrete beginning (start) and completion (stop) point separated by a relatively short time span.

Key schedule dates can be designated as milestones. Several types of dates might be chosen for use as milestones:

- Delivery of a significant output (i.e., system design, final report),
- Completion of a major task (i.e., develop instructional materials, select and train teachers),
- Major decision point (i.e., shall we fund this improvement next year?)

A milestone generally occasions a formal review of the status of costs and schedules and the success of implementation.

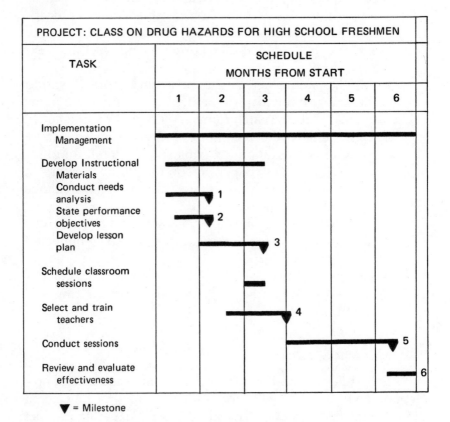

 = Milestone

FIGURE VI-4. A Typical Gantt Chart.

The Gantt chart is a common method for displaying a detailed work plan. A representative portion of a Gantt chart is shown in Figure VI-4.

The purpose of a Gantt chart is to provide the project director with a visual aid illustrating the time phasing and sequence of the various tasks associated with the project. Having this information, the director knows when and where to allocate resources to get the job done. It is known that one task must be complete before the beginning of another, if the second task requires the product of the first task before it can begin. Obviously, if the director wants to speed up the project, attempts should be made to run more tasks in parallel. This however, requires the use of more resources—especially manpower.

Special techniques exist which may provide assistance in the monitoring function, as well as in scheduling work, allocating resources, and in controlling time and costs. These techniques, such as Program Evaluation and Review Techniques (PERT) and Critical-Path (CP), call for organizing the information from the Gantt chart into a network flow graph in which the nodes represent target dates and other events, and in which the branches represent activities. Using the methods prescribed by these techniques the network may be analyzed for various purposes, such as to compute the probability that the task will be completed on schedule, or to locate the critical path through the network which prevents an earlier project completion date. Figure VI-5 is an example of a network diagram.

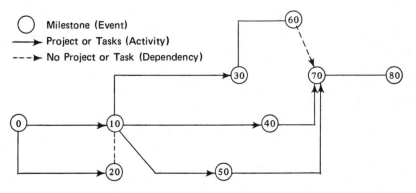

FIGURE VI-5. Example of Network Diagram.

Reporting

Reporting procedures must be planned to provide appropriate levels of management with necessary information to manage. This could mean detailed reports of accomplishment, schedules, and costs at the operating levels. At higher levels of management, reports that highlight progress are called for; but even then solely to the extent that the manager needs the information. Reports would normally cover the following aspects of implementation:

- Evaluation of accomplishments.
- Monitoring of costs and schedules.
- Identification of problems.
- Discussion of corrective action taken/advised.

The reporting system designed to meet the requirements described above should provide timely, understandable information, and should provide the basis for taking corrective actions. Monitoring of schedule and cost, for example, allows the following determinations to be made:

- Work progress.
- Reasons for slippage.
- Need for additional resources.
- Need for technical assistance.

Evaluation

An essential activity in the planning process is the evaluation of the degree to which implemented improvements are meeting their objectives.

Evaluation of accomplishment allows the following determinations to be made:

- Contribution of the improvement to stated goals and objectives.
- Need for additional resources.
- Desirability of alternative approaches.
- Reasons for lack of success.

The actual technique and methodologies for project evaluation are discussed in detail in the next chapter. The evaluation plan portion of the implementation plan described in this chapter refers to a plan for the allocation of project resources and activities to accomplish the selected evaluation methodology. The evaluation plan should contain:

- A description of the evaluation methodology to be used.
- Identification of the data that is to be collected.
- An indication as to who, how and when the data is to be collected and analyzed.
- A summation of the project resources to accomplish the evaluation.

This step concludes the description of the implementation planning process. In one sense, planning has been completed and the responsibility for implementation and operation is passed to the hands of the operational staff.

In a larger sense, however, what has been described is but one cycle of a process that, once started, should be continuously in action. For one thing, problems do not appear according to a neat annual cycle, an organization cannot afford to restrict planning to a process that begins in the spring and ends the following winter.

Practical implementation planning seldom follows precisely the orderly steps that have been used in this chapter; major problems and constraints are all subject to change.

Summary

The activities of implementation planning include:

- Strategy development
- Formation of a work plan, and
- Preparation of a reporting and evaluation plan.

As an implementation strategy is formulated the project expectations, organizational responsibilities, relationships and operational constraints must be clearly defined and understood between the policy and operational people concerned with the successful completion of the project. The methods for resource deployment and potential problem areas should also be identified and discussed.

The writing of a work plan requires the identification of the specific work tasks necessary to accomplish the project. From these tasks, budgets and milestone schedules can be prepared. A method for providing management feedback as to the project's progress and success in meeting the project objectives is covered in the preparation of the Reporting and Evaluation Plan.

Topics for Discussion

1. Discuss the importance of implementation strategy.
2. Briefly discuss the importance of a project director as a key person in the success of any project.
3. Discuss the project life cycle concept.
4. Draft a work plan for the burglary prevention project discussed in Chapter V.
5. Distinguish between goals, objectives and project expectation.
6. Differentiate between a Gantt Chart and a PERT or Critical-Path Chart.
7. Why should the reporting and evaluation plan be prepared before the project is implemented?

RESOURCE

IMPLEMENTATION PLAN FOR AN EDUCATION/
TRAINING DELIVERY SYSTEM

The study is subdivided into four phases, each representing a segment of the project having an output requiring project task force review, operational input, and approval. These four phases are:

I Project Plan and Data Collection

II Analysis of Training/Education Needs and Considerations

III Resource Center Design

IV Implementation Plan

Phase I sets the stage for the study and subsequent decision making. The importance of having everyone aware of the consequences of the study and collecting the correct data becomes obvious in later phases. Phase I accomplishes the initial orientation of the task force, the definition of study parameters, the development of a detailed work plan, the development of a data collection and analysis plan, and the survey of each of the criminal justice departments. At the conclusion of the data collection task, the survey team and the task force will meet to review the data collection process and validate the findings and preliminary resource center system descriptions developed during this phase of the study.

Phase II identifies general and specific criminal justice education and training requirements. Phase II includes describing the existing training and education systems of the three counties within the region, performing an analysis, and evaluating the delivery of criminal justice training and education. Current and proposed operational needs will be identified and compared to current efforts and resources. Research will be made into other experiences having occurred elsewhere relative to an education and training resource center. This analysis and description of current training and education systems and requirements will be utilized to develop a set of preliminary system specifications for a resource center. These system requirements and specifications will then be presented to the task force for review and, upon concurrence, the project team will establish a final set of design criteria.

Based on the previous activities, the project can now confidently enter the design phase. During Phase III we will develop a design for a resource center system that meets the immediate and long-range education and training needs, generates a program for developing manpower resources, and properly takes into account the external system interfaces with other institutions. This design will then be reviewed by the task force and a finalized design will be established during a task-force team design workshop.

These initial steps are to establish the roles of all the participants and to accomplish the orientation necessary to get the project off to a good start.

The acceptance of a final design for the criminal justice education/training system will be more likely if representatives of the departments participate in the development effort. It is recommended that the project task force act not only as a sounding board during the project, but also as an active participant in the analysis and design process. While not essential to the project, such project team participation in the design process could do much to ensure that the final work product is practical and useful.

A data gathering system will be developed for the project. The system will define the process for carrying out the identification, collection, validation and analysis of the project data. The process will involve the collection of all pertinent data directly from each criminal justice agency within the regions, as well as on-site surveys.

The emphasis of Phase IV is turning the agreed upon resource system design into a plan for action.

Phase IV includes formulating an implementation plan and preparing the final report which will be used to sell the design. A plan will be developed for implementing the recommended center including a grant proposal for funding. At the end of the project, a briefing of the project results will be presented to the task force.

It should be stressed that this approach requires strong involvement and input from representatives of the criminal justice agencies. In the long run, they are the users and must believe in the ultimate resource system. We have specified a number of points and specific tasks where criminal justice representatives are involved. In each of the four phases, there is active task force involvement. The remainder of this section discusses in detail the project task statements and methodology.

Phase I. Project Plan and Data Collection

Phase I is comprised of three tasks: finalizing a project plan, collecting relevant data from agencies and institutions in the regions as well as elsewhere in the state and nation, and preparing a description of the present delivery of criminal justice education and training. Phase I concludes with the review by the task force of the collected data and preliminary descriptions.

Task 1. Finalize Project Plan

The finalization of a project plan entails the accomplishment of five objectives.:

- Orienting Project Task Force Members
- Defining Study Parameters
- Developing a Data Collection/Analysis Plan
- Preparing a Detailed Work Plan

The data collection plan will set forth a system for surveying the criminal justice agencies, academic institutions, and similar projects to determine current operational practices and system needs for education and training. The data collection/survey vehicle will be specifically designed for this project.

Task 2. Data Collection

The data collection will consist of surveys and interviews to define current practices, trends, and future education and training needs.

The data collection is broken down into three areas:

- Operational Agency Survey
- Education (Academic) Survey
- Literature Search

OPERATIONAL AGENCY SURVEY

All agencies directly involved in or supportive of four counties' criminal justice systems will be surveyed and the results of that survey will form the primary information base for this study. The survey will address such subject areas as curriculum, facilities, personnel, demand for the resource center, available resources, and in-house expertise. Following are data required to accomplish this survey; other areas may be included as they are identified by staff and task force members:

- Determine all available pre-service and in-service education and training resources in Regions J and M.
  - The number of two-year, four-year, and university institutions within the region and locations.
  - Individual agency training programs (pre-performance, in-service, and special programs).
- Determine how many criminal justice personnel in the regions by occupational level and component.
  - Number of trainers within the regions and by component.
- Determine the level of training accomplished for each individual criminal justice employee.
  - POST training in the past three years for each of the criminal justice personnel.
  - Type and amount of training for each occupational level and component.
- Determine the recruitment and selection standards for each agency in the regions for all criminal justice personnel.
  - The entry level requirements for the criminal justice agencies.
- Determine the staff turnover rate for each criminal justice agency.
- Determine the expected organizational expansion for each agency in the next five years.
  - The manpower need beyond present staffing for each agency within the regions.
- Determine what provisions are made for criminal justice personnel in individual upgrading through education and training.

- ○ Incentives provided by the agency to encourage personnel to achieve additional higher education levels or training.
- • Determine education and training resource gaps.
  - ○ Lower divisions, upper divisions, and graduate programs needed in the regions.
  - ○ Special program needs such as management courses, courses for training officers, etc. (Identify where they are needed.)

EDUCATIONAL (ACADEMIC) SURVEY

During this portion of the data collection, colleges and universities in the regions will be contacted and provided with information relative to the project objectives. Discussions will be held with those institutions indicating an interest in affiliation, and affiliation recommendations will be made based on several considerations including mutual benefit, facilities, expertise, faculty, costs, and current college curriculum.

Substantial differences exist in the types and kinds of training and educational programs available to the members of each agency. The lengths of training periods, both at the entrance and advanced levels, differ drastically. Resources available to one agency are not available to or used by the others and, more often than not, are not even known to exist.

There are similar positions existing in two or more agencies of the criminal justice system. The position incumbents, despite their similarity of functions, seldom receive the same educational-training treatment after satisfaction of pre-employment requirements.

This survey study will identify existing areas of training-education curriculum duplication, areas of mutual concern presently void of curriculum, new system needs in terms of curriculum (general criminal justice system knowledge may be one system-wide need), and existing curriculum that appears non-compatible or required in only one agency or system component.

The result of the education study will be curriculum recommendations relative to training-education of all criminal justice system personnel utilizing the resource center concept of network resources and maximum interaction. Curriculum recommendations will be reviewed by the task force and by others possessing expertise in particular system disciplines.

LITERATURE SEARCH

This portion of the data collection effort will focus on the experiences of other training/education resource centers. The specific information to be produced from this effort covers the following areas:

- centralized vs. decentralized operation
- sources of funding
- affiliation
- administrative coordination
- Project STAR
- National Standards and Goals

The literature search will cover areas which presently have the resource center concept in operation. The anticipated centers to be contacted are located at the following geographic areas:

1. Issaquah, Washington
2. Honolulu, Hawaii
3. Independence, Missouri
4. New York, New York
5. Modesto, California
6. Oroville, California
7. Santa Barbara/Ventura, California

As the surveys are conducted, a set of preliminary education and training system descriptions will be developed to portray the survey team's understanding and perception of the current criminal justice requirements.

These surveys will result in an overview of the entire system and provide information relative to the objectives and operations of the various system components.

Further, an intensive study of the planning board's staff documents, planning board member and staff inputs, and personal interviews with the executives and staffs of agencies operating within the two regions will be added to the information base for the regional information gathering effort. The information gleaned from these sources will be reviewed and discussed by the project staff and by experts in the various training-professional disciplines. Armed with this information, the task force can begin to draw logical conclusions regarding the existing types and levels of training and education in each component of the system, determine existing and future needs of component, and identify appropriate areas of mutual concern and interface. A series of recommendations can begin to be formulated relative to the resource center and the regional needs, including but not limited to consideration of such issues as centralization vs. decentralization, administration, curriculum, personnel, funding, participation, etc.

Task 3 Project Task Force Review of Data Collection Task and Initial Description of Current Education/Training Systems Programs

At the conclusion of the data collection phase, the survey team and the project task force will meet to review the data collection process and initial description of current education and training systems and informational findings from the surveys. This meeting will include a general orientation followed by detailed discussions concerning the findings. At least a day should be set aside for this effort.

Phase II Analysis of Training/Education Needs and Considerations

Phase II of the project will entail the systematic description and analysis of the existing training/education systems, the identification of user education and training requirements, the development of a preliminary set of criminal resource center specifications, a review of the descriptions and specifications by the project task force and a project team design workshop to establish the specific design criteria and specifications of the education/training center.

Task 4 Analysis of Existing Systems

The information from the surveys of the criminal justice agencies and external agencies will be further analyzed to determine the nature, characteristics, and scope of the present education/
training systems in the regions. The review and comments from the task force meeting coupled with additional data where necessary will form the basis of this analysis. Projections will be prepared providing data to assist in determining future needs.

Because of the variations in delivery services, training needs are separated from educational needs. This division may be arbitrary and unworkable. If so, this will become known during the course of the project.

The important aspect of this task is getting beyond what is presently being carried out into the area of user requirements. Training needs will be classified into various categories such as subject matter, repetitiveness, etc. These requirements must include resources necessary to meet the needs.

Task 5 Establish Preliminary Specifications for a Criminal Justice Resource Center

The information developed in Task 4 will be translated into a set of preliminary specifications for a resource center concept. These specifications will identify training and education requirements and demands in terms of resources which would be required from a resource center. PSi will also look at feasible alternative designs which will meet the regions' needs in this task. These specifications cover administrative control, instructional services, and staffing.

Task 6 Task Force Workshop

The completion of Phase II involves an extensive review of the work done to date by the project task force and project team. The workshop will be divided into two parts, the first is the review and approval of resource center specifications, and the second is the formulation of criteria for the resource center design. The products of Phase II will be reviewed by the project team. Discrepancies will be identified and adjusted. Descriptions, requirements, and preliminary resource system specifications will be used to form a set of project design criteria which will guide staff in Phase III.

Phase III Conceptual Resource Center Design

A criminal justice resource center design and recommended description will be constructed in Phase III. A workshop will be used to finalize the criminal justice resource center design.

Task 7 Resource Center Design

The success of the entire project rests with the completion of this task. The understanding of the resource system concept, local conditions, and other factors completed earlier in the project culminates in this task. The conceptual design is based on considerable in-depth analysis and requires substantial feedback from the ultimate users.

The beginning point in completing the resource center design is identifying and developing the various practical alternative designs. Some design will come about by the results of the Literature Search undertaken in Task 2. Other designs will be identified during work in the regions. Each of these alternatives will be developed in sufficient detail to allow for critical review and evaluation. Particular emphasis will focus on facility requirements, organizational and operational requirements, and staffing requirements.

COST ANALYSIS

Each design alternative will be costed out for implementation and first-year operation of the resource center. Costs will be determined based on curriculum, facility, affiliation, personnel, administration, equipment recommendations, overhead, etc. These analyses include identifying possible cost savings by using existing facilities, etc. A part of the ultimate design will use these analyses.

A major effort of this task is determining funding sources. It would appear that the principal source of initial capital outlay would have to come from ADA and grants. Annual operating costs could be partially supported by federal funds for several years, but ultimately the state and particpating agencies would be required to take over total funding. Another possibility that must be explored is the implication of Senate Bill (SB) 90, "Property Tax Relief Act of 1972," which has provisions for making subventions to local government agencies to carry out state programs.

Part of the funding problem is determining the manner in which local users would be obligated to support the final resource design. Assessment, quota, rates, and other methods will be identified and evaluated.

Task 8 Task Force Workshop

The task force team will be reassembled for a review of the various resource center designs. PSi will provide an in-depth explanation of the details of each alternative design. The task force will use the criteria developed in Task 6 to evaluate each alternative. Upon completion of this evaluation, a design workshop will be carried out to establish a final recommended system.

Phase IV Implementation Plan and Final Report

The final phase of the project will produce details of the final resource system design, an implementation plan, and the final report. The final report will be designed to be used as a grant request for funding the resource center.

Task 9 Prepare Implementation Plan

The implementation plan as conceived by the team is an action plan. Included in the plan are the specific details of the regional criminal justice resource system, the specific requirements (organizational, procedural and content, manpower, and facilities and equipment), and schedule for implementing the system with accompanying costs. A separate section of the plan addresses the potential political and legal constraints and needs. The implementation plan will be the document used by the task force members to inform and obtain agreement from user agencies and various local government officials. The plan will contain the following sections:

ORGANIZATIONAL REQUIREMENTS

This section of the implementation plan will indicate the type of organizational structure the resource center will have. Specific points covered in this section include:

- Organization Structure and Hierarchy
- User Advisory Committee
- Educational Institutions Liaison
- Evaluation and Control
- Support Services

PROCEDURAL AND TRAINING/EDUCATION REQUIREMENTS

This section spells out procedures, methodology and course description. Subjects covered under procedures and methodology include:

- Scheduling
- Coordination
- Facility and equipment usage
- Instructional services
- Instructional methodology

Material under course description provides the foundation for the detailed curriculum content. Specific discussion will be provided for:

- Training area needs
- Education area needs
- Course objectives
- Course subject area
- Course sources and resources

This section will document the curriculum content of basic courses, advanced and refresher courses, integrated criminal justice courses, specialized and technical courses.

MANPOWER REQUIREMENTS

This section delineates the staffing needed to operate the criminal justice resource center. The material covered in this section includes:

- Qualifications and selection criteria
- Permanent/temporary staff
- Community resources and availability
- Evaluation

The important factors covered in developing manpower needs will have some documentation included in the previous section.

EQUIPMENT AND FACILITIES

The documentation of the physical facilities and equipment needed to operate the criminal justice resource center is an important factor. If the center is defined as an institution with the primary objective of providing instructional resources —teaching personnel, library, audio-visual equipment and material, consultants, etc. for the use of criminal justice agencies at their locations, the physical facilities must be flexible. Perhaps, a central facility location with the use of an education/training van would provide a centralized base with the added advantage of decentralized capability. Further, the type of equipment needed to accomplish this objective will be documented.

The next step in Task 9 is preparing the implementation specifics including a time-phased schedule, a budget, and a listing of possible political and legal constraints. Along with this implementation plan the criminal justice and government officials can begin to take steps to assure all activity is completed in a logical manner.

IMPLEMENTATION SCHEDULE

The importance of proper scheduling is obvious. This sub-task will identify and describe each event in terms of its objectives, methodology, and resources needed for completion, and listing output products. The interrelationship between events will be clearly identified along with the critical path necessary to accomplish implementation. The implementation schedule will be made part of the final report. It will be used in preparing a grant proposal.

IMPLEMENTATION COSTS

No plan is complete without knowledge of the costs involved. This information is vital for decision making, planning present expenditures, and preparing future budgets. Decisions made in previous tasks relative to funding will be incorporated in this plan. Among the cost figures will be:

- Facilities (new remodeling or whatever is necessary)
- Capital outlay equipment
- Supplies
- Library and reference documents
- Salaries
- Operating expenses
- Other costs

IDENTIFICATION OF POLITICAL AND LEGAL CONSIDERATIONS

This sub-task will assist and smooth the way for implementation. The effect of this portion of the report is to uncover possible pitfalls that may cause implementation difficulty. The plan will document the possible political constraints which might have some impact. This will entail looking at the following areas:

- Agency-oriented constraints (people)
- District/county/city relationships
- Special district controls
- Single municipal control

This sub-task will also look at the various legal ramifications in the area of funding. This includes but is not limited to:

- Federal Government (LEAA)
- HEW
- OCJP
- Operational Agencies
- Counties
- POST
- State Board of Education

Task 10 Prepare Final Report

The project will be culminated with a final report. This document will contain a statement of resource center requirements and specifications, a description of the recommended system, any applicable alternatives, and the implementation plan.

This task will culminate with a formal briefing and presentation to the project task force.

REFERENCES

Adams, Thomas, *Criminal Justice Organization and Management*, Pacific Palasades, California: Goodyear Publishing Co., 1974. A discussion of the agencies that make up the Criminal Justice System with emphasis on managerial issues. Chapter 8—Research and Planning for Effectiveness—is particularly useful.

A Guide for Criminal Justice Planning, a booklet produced by the California Council on Criminal Justice, 1971, 67 pp. A guide used by the California State Planning Agency and Regional Planning Units for the preparation of their 1971 comprehensive criminal justice system plans.

Ewing, David, Editor, *Long Range Planning for Management*, New York: Harper and Row, 1972. A book of readings on selected planning issues by noted professionals. The book is business oriented, however, concepts are applicable to criminal justice.

Hall, Arthur D., *A Methodology for Systems Engineering*, New Jersey, Van Nostrand Company, Inc., 1962, p. 456. The subject of this book is the methodology or process of systems engineering, with its contents of tools, case histories and history of the field.

Schoderbek, Peter, Asterios Keplas and Charles Schoderkek, *Management Systems: Conceptual Considerations*, Dallas, Texas: Business Publications Inc., 1975. A general management text on systems theory, useful material relative to implementation and planning for information systems.

Chapter Objectives

1. Establishes the need for pre-approval review.
2. Develops an understanding of review and evaluation guidelines.
3. Promote an understanding of evaluation guidelines.
4. Describes impact completion evaluation.
5. Identifies the four basic components of evaluation.
6. Develops an understanding of program control.
7. Describes the process of setting goals and objectives as integral components of evaluation.
8. Presents an evaluation design.

7
Evaluation

Pre-approval review and impact completion evaluation are crucial, but often overlooked components of successful program management. The quality of these review/evaluation activities is of such importance that more and more managers are coming to realize the benefits to be derived from seeing that they are performed well.

Specifically, this chapter will address the question of what is the management process, particularly as it relates to evaluation in the criminal justice environment. It will also discuss the need for both pre-approval review and impact completion evaluation as the crucial evaluation components related to the four discernable components, namely:

- Setting goals and objectives
- Program planning
- Program control
- Impact completion evaluation

Most managers perform some type of program evaluation. What they would like to do is improve the use of evaluation as a management tool. The problem is that a certain mystique now surrounds the evaluation process—particularly in the public sector. This has been partly caused by university-trained academic-theoretical oriented individuals. They were not familiar with real operational agency problems and typically used Student's T Tests, Fisher's F and multiple linear regression as a means of communicating their evaluation of results.

Another problem with evaluation has been that the word itself has gained a certain negative connotation. This has occured primarily because of fallout from some early evaluation projects in which emphasis was placed on finding fault with the concept of the program—after the fact—instead of evaluating whether the program achieved its stated objectives.

There is an urgent need to ensure a better understanding of the evaluation process by appropriate managers and operating personnel. Once this basic understanding has been achieved, it will be much less difficult to design and implement evaluation components as part of projects undertaken.

A recent publication, on evaluation research in corrections, (Cooper, 1975) suggests that evaluation be defined as "a procedure for ascertaining whether an event, process, or situation (real or conceptualized) is better than another. The procedure may include steps for measuring 'how much better' and for explaining the reasons for the difference."

This definition provides a good base for understanding impact-completion evaluation, but does not address the evaluation environment. The remainder of this chapter will attempt to shed light on evaluation as an integral part of the planning process.

Components of Evaluation—Setting Goals and Objectives

Each program begins as a concept of a desired result. Generally, the concept is expressed in very broad terms. It is the job of the manager to define, as clearly as possible, the specific goal. Examples of goals:

- Reduce criminal justice processing time of offenders.
- Improve up-time of street maintenance vehicles.
- Decrease turn-around time in handling citizens' complaints.

The next step is to relate specific objectives to the goal. Generally, objectives should be more definitive statements of the goal. There are usually one or more objectives associated with each goal. The objectives, being more specific, provide the basis for establishing limits (response times, money, personnel levels, etc.) for the program. They also describe the benefits to be obtained.

Stated objectives also serve another important purpose. Objectives provide the logical departure point for developing measures of performance for evaluating program results (Cooper, 1975). Since objectives relate to program results, statistical measures of performance are similarly related to objectives. Examples of objectives:

- Primary Importance: Objective 1—Reduce the criminal justice processing time of offenders by ten days within the next year.
- Secondary Importance: Objective 2—Increase the recovery rate of total dollar value loss in burglaries by 10% over last year's.

As can be seen by the above two examples, we have not even started to discuss programs for accomplishment of our objectives. It is also quite possible to have several primary objectives and several secondary objectives. Each one must be articulated. Emphasis is placed on the manager's awareness of objectives and the priorities that should be assigned to them.

Program Planning

Once the goal(s) and objectives of a program have been defined, the next step is to express these goals and objectives in terms of the activities which must be taken to achieve the desired results. These activities are referred to as programs of action.

Each program can be defined in terms of one or more projects. A single project may be directed at achieving a specific objective, or several programs and/or projects may be designed to jointly serve one objective. In some cases a certain program may be directed at achieving more than one of the objectives. A problem in evaluation is: How do you isolate which program accomplished the objective?

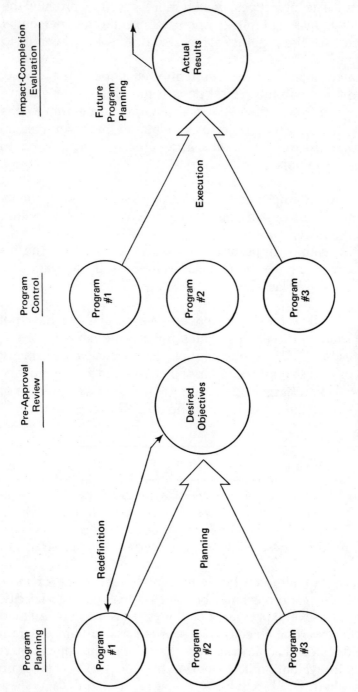

FIGURE VII-1. Program Planning Review.

Program development is the basic planning step in the program management process. It defines the needed resources and asseses whether they are available in order to meet the required goal(s) and objectives.

When objectives and programs are merged into a model, the impetus for review and evaluation is clear. This is illustrated in Figure VII-1.

Pre-approval review is the first half of the two-part review/evaluation process. As shown in Figure VII-1 it is the last activity associated with the program planning process. Post-completion evaluation, the last activity of the program execution process, is described later.

Pre-approval review consists of the following basic activities:

- Review (with the program team) the program's stated goal(s) and objectives for clarity and agreement.
- Assess whether the real problem, or only its symptoms, have been defined.
- Review the proposed program's structures.
- Assess whether the proposed programs appear to be practical activities designed to achieve the stated goal(s) and objectives.
- Review the work plans for the various programs.
- Assess the feasibility of the work plans in terms of the manpower, money, materials and time constraints involved.
- Review the level of training and experience of program management in the basic techniques of program direction and control.
- Assess whether a sufficient level of program management training and experiences exists to successfully guide this particular program.

There is one other element in the program planning process which has been deliberately left until last in order to highlight it. This is the need for management to develop and agree on objective measures of performance by which the results of the program may be judged. Use of performance measures is the best way to implement the management-by-objectives concept in program management. Through the establishment of performance measures, management quantifies its goals and objectives in advance.

What is often missed is the fact that unless performance measures or criteria are set up and agreed to by the project team before a program begins, it is extremely difficult for the post-completion evaluator to accurately audit the results. Of equal importance is another fact—unless the program manager agrees to these evaluation criteria before the program begins, the report of the post-completion evaluation may be rejected by him as having missed the mark.

Performance measures are quantitative in nature and of three types:

- Financial indicators.
- Statistical (i.e., non-financial) indicators.
- Milestone completion targets (time frame and tasks)

Program costs must be compared to the program budget on the account-by-account basis. The slippage of tasks completed could cause a program severe problems in terms of finances and completion.

Here are some examples of performance measures/criteria which have been used by project managers in conducting certain criminal justice projects:

- Criminal justice agency feasibility.
- Costs.
- Time frame.
- Manpower required.
- Agency capability.
- Political feasibility.
- Ease of operation.
- Social feasibility.

The *evaluation methodology* includes the *techniques* of evaluation and answers four important questions:

- *Who* will do the evaluation?
- *When* will the evaluation take place?

- *Where* will the evaluation take place?
- *How* will the evaluation take place?

The first question necessitates a decision on whether the evaluation will be done by the agency itself, a consultant, etc. The second question poses the timing of the evaluation taking place: at the beginning of the program, continuously throughout the program, or at the end of the program. The third question deals with location of the evaluation effort. If it is done by an agency, will it be done by planning and research, school campus facility, or others? The fourth and last question deals with the specific technique of evaluation. Namely, will one use a subjective questionnaire, computer analysis, or simple statistics collected? The criminal justice manager will probably not know the answers to these evaluation methodology questions, but he should be aware of them. They are endlessly recurring regardless of the nature of evaluation.

Management, therefore, must propose the criteria or performance measures with which it feels it would like to be judged in terms of successfully achieving a program's stated goals and objectives. The pre-approval reviewer must independently assess whether he believes there are fair, relevant and practical measures for use by the manager in guiding the program as well as the post-completion evaluator in assessing results.

Pre-approval review, which closes off the planning stage of a program, has a built-in feedback mechanism which must be satisfied before program execution can begin. If as a result of the review the manager feels weaknesses still exist in any of the areas appraised, recommendations should be made to the granting agency that the program team return to its planning mode and resubmit its program application.

The discussion thus far has only dealt with evaluating a *single program* against one or more *objectives* by a set of *criteria* utilizing a specific *evaluation methodology*. This evaluation scheme as presented, does not assume existence of alternatives. If alternative programs exist, and this is common, one has to be able to determine which alternative program is most appropriate. Thus, the need for prioritizing program selection.

In making a comparison, for example Programs A and B, it is absolutely *vital* to recognize that an accurate and meaningful evaluation is impossible if different criteria, evaluation methodologies, or objectives are used. Simply, Program A and Program B cannot be evaluated, one against the other, if objectives are changed or if different sets of criteria or evaluation methodologies are used. A simplistic guideline can be established in the evaluation for the purpose of comparing programs. Of the evaluation components, (objectives, programs, criteria, and evaluation methodologies), *only program* may be varied; everything else must remain *constant.* In summary, programs cannot be compared if different objectives, criteria, and methodologies are used. A model for comparing two or more programs is depicted in Figure VII-2.

When alternative programs are evaluated against the same objectives, using common criteria and the same evaluation methodology, a determination as to which program is the better of the alternatives is made by the use of two *factors.* Factor one is a simple determination as to which program *best meets* the objectives. The second factor deals with the criteria and how each program *measures up* against the criteria. This has been discussed in detail in Chapter VI.

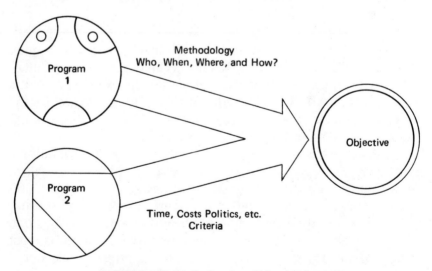

FIGURE VII-2. Evaluation Objective Impact.

Program Control

The program manager, having set goal(s) and objectives, established programs of action, undergone pre-approval review and received program funding, is now ready to energize the program. To assemble the designated program team, institute financial and administrative procedures, obtain facilities and supplies and deposit program funds, are necessary tasks.

During the execution phase, the manager's job is one of direction, coordination and control. This is the stage when the highest use of interpersonal skills is made. One must monitor the use of resources according to plan and hold frequent reviews to determine whether program activities are accomplishing desired results or whether certain activities (or indeed the entire program) must be altered to keep the program on track.

For assistance in this process the manager needs a program control system. Such a system should include the following elements:

- Budgetary control (i.e., financial plan or budget, periodic reporting of actual expenditures compared to budgeted amounts on an account-by-account and program-by-program basis, etc.)
- Status reporting (i.e., periodic reporting of accomplishments according to the work plan and in terms of the pre-established measures of performance.)
- Progress meetings (i.e., periodic meetings of the manager with the project staff to discuss progress in terms of the budget(s), work plan and indicated performance.)

The most important aspect of program control is that it needs to be formalized. Seat-of-the-pants management may be an art, but consistently good results in program management are achieved by managers who utilize a structured approach based on modern management techniques.

The adequacy of the program control system in relation to the program it is designed to control is one of the important factors assessed in the pre-approval review process.

After execution of the program is completed, the manager should evaluate results. Actually, if the program control system has been used properly, the post-completion evaluation is merely the last in a series of similar program reviews to be conducted throughout the life of the program.

If the program control system has functioned properly, the manager knows on the last day of the program whether or not, according to expert judgment, the program has achieved its goal(s). In other words, at the close of the program, has each activity met the objectives established for the program?

Post-completion evaluation for the manager, then, should actually be future-oriented in the sense that the manager should use this time to assess the knowledge received from the results achieved in terms of applicability to future programs.

There is another aspect to post-completion evaluation, however; this is the second-level evaluation which should be conducted by the same outside review-evaluation team which handled the pre-approval review function. The reviewer (or review team) who conducted the pre-approval review should now follow through and conduct the post-completion evaluation.

It has been emphasized in the discussion thus far that if all the other planning and control steps of the program management process have been properly followed, post-completion evaluation can be significantly reduced from its normal scope. This is chiefly because of the front-end review function built into the process at the pre-approval review stage.

It also results from the fact that financial/statistical indicators of performance were established during the planning process so that the manager can now focus efforts during the post-completion evaluation stage on whether reported results indicate that the expected goal(s) and objectives were achieved. What has happened all too frequently in the past is, the evaluator has had to make up criteria (many of which were subjective and qualitative in nature) after the fact. This is not only inefficient and time consuming, it can also be counterproductive if the manager of the program does not agree that the criteria selected accurately measure results.

The crucial elements of pre-approval review and impact completion evaluation are the activities which harmonize the management process and provide the ultimate credibility to the success of the program. Often they constitute the crucial difference in successful program management, particularly in the case of programs funded with federal/state grants.

The above evaluation model has discussed the components of setting goals and objectives, program planning, program control and impact-completion evaluation. It is well recognized that within each component, a complex set of interaction takes place. Many of these specific interactions, i.e. data collection and analysis, have been discussed in previous chapters.

Summary

The evaluation process should be viewed by the criminal justice manager as an integral part of the operation. A guide prepared under an LEAA grant (Evaluation in Criminal Justice Programs: Guidelines and Examples, 1973, p. 15) suggests that the managerial review should accomodate the following:

1. *Statement of Goals and Objectives:* Does the evaluation component offer a clear statement of the goals or objectives of the project? Goals or objectives are simply summary statements highlighting what the project is designed to achieve. In order to be most useful, they should attempt to quantify desired results. As such, they provide the basis both for the evaluation planning and the evaluational analysis surrounding the project.
2. *Identification of Evaluation Measures:* Does the evaluation component clearly identify those measures appropriate to the project's stated goals or objectives? A project's goals or objectives are the key to the development of the overall evaluation component. Hence, the evaluation measures appropriate to a given project should correlate with the project's goals.
3. *Specification of Data Requirements:* Does the evaluation component exhaustively specify the data required for

developing the evaluation measures? Data from a variety of sources and dealing with diverse aspects of a project will often be required to form a single evaluation measure. The specification of data requirements, therefore, involves the explicit determination of the data elements required for the evaluation.

4. *Statement of Data Collection Approach:* Does the evaluation component state how the required data will be collected? Responsibility should be assigned for reporting various required data elements. Specific reporting periods ought to be established, and designs for simplified, standardized forms should be included.

5. *Statement of the Data Analysis Approach:* Does the evaluation component present a data analysis plan? The project goals or objectives and their associated evaluation measures must motivate any data analysis efforts. The analysis plan, then, should summarize how the data elements are to be combined to determine project results.

6. *Presentation of Evaluation Reporting Schedule:* Does the evaluation component present an appropriate evaluation reporting schedule both in terms of report content and timing? The successful results of programs are oftentimes determined by how well a manager performs his responsibilities for program evaluation.

An example evaluation design for an LEAA project (High Impact Anti-Crime Program Sample, July 1974, U.S. Department of Justice Law Enforcement Assistance Administration National Institute of Law Enforcement and Criminal Justice) is presented in the resource section of this chapter.

Topics for Discussion

1. Discuss the importance of evaluation.
2. Describe the relationship of goals and objectives to the evaluation process.
3. Briefly describe program control.

4. Discuss the use of impact evaluation in criminal justice agencies.
5. Describe the steps necessary to prepare a viable evaluation component to a project or program.
6. Discuss the value of pre-approval review to the evaluation process.

RESOURCE

EVALUATION DESIGN

Newark Project Summary

Project Title: Special Case Processing for Impact Offenders

Grant Number: 73-DF-02-0101

Project Objective: To reduce by 45% the amount of time it presently takes to process offenders charged with Impact crimes, from arrest through sentence.

Projector Director: James Giuliano, Assistant Judge (temporary appointment until appointment of Assistant Court Administrator)

Host Agency: Assistant Court Administrator
Essex County Court House
Newark, New Jersey

Date of Award: 26 June 1973

Period of Award: July 15, 1973–July 14, 1974

Funding: Federal Share: $474,777
      Local Share: $225,189
      Total Project Amount $699,966

This project proposes to improve the overall quality of justice within the adjudication process through procedural changes and supplemental personnel. This will include modifications in the entire process from the Municipal Court arraignment through County Court sentencing and will stress three courts designated to hear only Impact offenders, decrease the present workload and prepare the court system for the potential increase in arrests due to the implementation of other Impact projects.

Project Description

The project proposes to establish an IMPACT-Crime Court process that will utilize select resources of the adjudication system to deal only with court cases involving IMPACT offenders. Specifically, additional prosecutors, public defenders, three judges, investigators, and clerks will be coordinated by an Assistant Court Administrator (reporting to the Essex County Assignment Judge) for the purpose of reducing the amount of time it presently takes to process IMPACT offenders from arrest through sentence by 45%. Concurrently, it will attempt to reduce the process time for all offenders by 10%, and improve the overall quality of justice within the adjudication process.

These objectives will be pursued by modifying procedures and supplementing personnel in the existing Newark-Essex courts system. These modifications will take place throughout the process (Municipal Court arraignment through County Court sentencing) and will center around three existing courts designated to hear only IMPACT complaints.

Project Objectives

Performance Objectives

1. To complete the adjudication process from arrest to sentencing for Newark offenders charged with IMPACT crimes within 90 days and as close to 60 days as possible (45% reduction over present time).
2. To achieve collateral benefits throughout the Newark-Essex court system, reducing over-all delays by 10%.
3. To achieve crime prevention benefits from the court process by arriving at a judicial determination in close proximity to the commission of the crime thereby reducing the amount of re-arrests prior to sentencing.
4. To improve the overall quality of justice within the judicial process.

Capability Objectives

1. To provide the municipal court the resources and supportive personnel necessary to rapidly process and refer complaints involving IMPACT crimes.
2. To provide the county courts the resources and supportive personnel necessary to complete the adjudication process through sentencing within 90 days.

Baseline Data

Projected Number of Cases

The Newark Crime Analysis Team IMPACT target crime survey (see IMPACT Action Plan, appendix) revealed that a definitive percentage of the total number of person-to-person target offenders were stranger-to-stranger. These percentages were applied to the number of complaints received by the Newark Municipal Court (1972), complaints referred to the Grand Jury indictments returned to arrive at a projected caseload level of 710. In tabular format:

COMPLAINTS (ARRESTS) RECEIVED BY THE
NEWARK MUNICIPAL COURT

All Offenses		*Stranger to Stranger**	
Murder	130	25	(19%)
Rape	178	103	(58%)
Robbery	1337	976	(73%)
AA & B	1379	427	(31%)
B & E	1754	1754	(100%)
TOTALS	4478	3285	

Percentages taken from a survey of Impact offenses during a period from June 1971-May 1972.

COMPLAINTS REFERRED TO GRAND JURY FROM NEWARK

All Offenses		Stranger to Stranger
Murder	111	21
Rape	130	75
Robbery	899	656
AA & B	894	277
B & E	523	523
TOTALS	2557	1552

INDICTMENTS RETURNED
(80% OF TOTAL COUNTY FIGURE)

All Offenses		Stranger to Stranger
Murder	62	12
Rape	53	31
Robbery	513	373
AA & B	222	69
B & E	225	225
TOTALS	1075	710

Current Timetable–Indicatable Offenses;
Newark/Essex Court System

The following narrative presents time (in court days) from an arrest to a sentencing for a typical indictable offense under current conditions.

The municipal court is the first component of the judicial process to deal with the complaints in question. Arraignment is usually within 24 hours and usually, if the charge is substantiated, it will merely be referred to the Prosecutor for presentation before the Grand Jury. Preliminary hearings, while taking place in less than 50% of the cases, must be considered and usually take place 7 days after arraignment.

10 days   Another day will be spent getting the complaint to the Prosecutor's office.

1 day   Another day will be spent once the complaint arrives at the Prosecutor's office in the normal course of sorting and redirecting the mail. Eventually it will be given to the pre-Grand Jury squad.

14 days	The pre-Grand Jury squad must prepare the cases for presentation to the Grand Jury. This requires obtaining arrest reports from the police department along with the follow-up reports and establishing witness lists and drawing up subpoenas. Two weeks is required to accomplish this.
30 days	The present number of cases allows for complaints which are ready for Grand Jury presentation to be scheduled about one month ahead. During this one-month period, subpoenas are served by special Sheriff's squad.
7 days	If the Grand Jury returns an indictment, it will be presented to the Assignment Judge on the following Thursday. All indictments are presented on the same day so some will have been returned in a shorter time than others, but a one-week delay is average.
7 days	The Criminal Court Clerk must schedule these cases for arraignment (pleading) and prepares notices of appearance. The arraignment date is usually set one week ahead.

Pleas at arraignment are almost universally not guilty so a trial date must be set. Also, at this time, defense counsel is usually formally assigned after court petition. Trials are usually scheduled about one week away. |
| 40 days | Experience shows that many times defense cannot be prepared so rapidly and along with various pre-trial motions, 40 days is actually required. If a defendant is found guilty or if during this month a guilty plea is entered, a sentencing is done once a month, another 30 days will be necessary till the case is finally disposed. |
| 30 days | If a defendant is found guilty or if during this month a guilty plea is entered, a sentencing day must be established. Since sentencing is done once a month, another 30 days will be necessary till the case is finally disposed. |

It can be estimated, therefore, that present procedures allow for processing in around 139 days. Just as it is evident the courts alone are not responsible for this time lag, neither can the assignment of special courts to IMPACT offenses alone meet the stipulated objectives. Procedures also must be modified. The mechanism in its present form will not allow for a 60-90 day process.

Proposed Versus Current Court Timetable

Described below is the proposed court timetable vis a vis the current. Notice the project entails procedural as well as staffing changes.

Evaluation Measures

Measures of Effectiveness

1. Median* length of time in court days it takes IMPACT offender from arrest to sentencing. The absolutely critical measure of effectiveness is the amount of time it takes the offender to be processed through the "IMPACT Court" process. A special reporting form (see attached) has been developed which will document dates as well as length of time (in court days) each step in the process takes. It is envisioned that the prosecuting attorney will complete each form (for each case he processes) and submit it to the project director after the sentencing date. The project director will be the focal point of the collection of these reporting forms and will clip-off the names of the offenders (to assure confidentiality) when submitting the forms to IMPACT. Note that by employing such a reporting form, evaluators can pinpoint *where* delays, if any, are occurring in the system.

2. Median* length of time—other courts. It is not clear at this time how this data will be procured. It is en-

---

"Median" is utilized to discount the effects of an "outlier" value, i.e., one that is either so high or low as to make the average shift significantly one direction or the other.

visioned, however, that the project director will sample data available from the prosecutor's office to account for collateral time reduction benefits brought about by the implementation of special IMPACT courts.

3. Number (%) of first offenders processed through the Court.

Number (%) of second, third, . . .offenders processed through the court.

While this measure has no direct bearing on the evaluation of time reduction benefits of this project, it is a critically important piece of data to collect. Such a measure will provide IMPACT evaluators with a current assessment of recidivism processed through the Court. While this measure has no direct bearing on the evaluation of time reduction benefits of this project, it is a critically important piece of data to collect. Such a measure will provide IMPACT evaluators with a current assessment of recidivism processed through the Court.

This measure has important uses for the evaluation of other IMPACT projects and hence will be collected here.

4. The number (%) of target offenders processed through the Court who are re-arrested before sentencing (by type of arrest)

The importance of this measure is to account for any crime reduction benefits accrued to the speediness of the adjudication process; that is, does an inverse relationship exist between time spent in adjudication and number of re-arrests before sentencing? This data will emanate from two sources—the IMPACT Case Tracking system (described below) as well as the reporting form attached below.

Measures of Efficiency

1. General
   a. The number (%) target offender cases placed on bail.

b. The number (%) target offender cases placed in ROR status.
c. The number (%) of target offender cases detained after arraignment.

(all Monthly)

d. The number (%) of target offender cases which involve individuals participating or previously participating in another IMPACT program.

(Quarterly—estimate)

The above three measures are important determinants in providing information as to how the system is operating. Item (c), is especially significant because it ties in with the IMPACT Case Tracking System described below. Since each IMPACT participant will be given a special IMPACT number, (and that will identify him to a particular program) careful accounting must be assured so that the participant is not given another IMPACT number via the Court program. Only first-offenders and non-IMPACT participants should receive IMPACT numbers via the Court program. ROR status will be subdivided by the type of program (if any) to which the defender has been diverted.

2. By Process
a. Number of cases reviewed by Complaint and Indictment Section (monthly)
b. Number of cases brought before Municipal Court arraignment (monthly)
c. Number of cases for which there is a preliminary hearing (monthly)
d. Number of cases presented to Grand Jury (monthly)
e. Number of target offender cases where indictment by Grand Jury is sent down (monthly)
f. Number of target offender cases where the Grand Jury presents no bills
g. Number of target offender cases assigned to each IMPACT Court (monthly)

h. Number of target offender pleadings (arraignment) "not guilty" before IMPACT judge (monthly)
i. Number of target offender "guilty" pleadings before IMPACT judge (monthly)
j. Document Sentencing for these guilty cases (special reporting format)—# of offenders in each sentencing alternative; median length of sentenced time
k. Number of target offender trials held (monthly)
l. Number of target offender guilty verdicts
m. Number of target offender not guilty verdicts
n. Number of guilty offenders x sentencing alternative
o. Median length of time for these sentences. The above fifteen measures will be gathered in the special reporting form and/or the IMPACT Performance Management System (PMS) reporting forms (described below). They will be analyzed along various dimensions (example: comparison of the sentences of first versus second, third. . .offenders, number of indictments handed down by grand jury first versus second, third. . .offenders and so on).

3. Offender Data
   a. Number of Newark residents charged (special reporting form)
   b. Number of offenders charged by type of IMPACT crime (forcible rape, robbery, atrocious assault and battery and B & E) as well as a determination of the victim-offender relationship—(special reporting form)The purpose of these measures is to provide an assessment of the type of cases (by crime) as well as the "source" of the offender. This latter data element is particularly important because it provides some indication of a crime displacement factor (non-residents committing crime in Newark) possibly existing in Newark.

4. Additudinal Measures
   a. Judges
   b. Prosecutors

c. Public Defenders

One of the objectives of the project (and in some ways a constraint to speedy process) is to improve the overall quality of justice. Interviews developed by the CAT in conjunction with the Project Director will be conducted to gain some understanding of this element. The interviews, to occur at most every six months, will seek to discover:

- The relative quality of defense preparation
- The relative quality of prosecution's case
- Satisfaction concerning pleas
- Assessment of sentencing
- The overall effectiveness of a special case processing concept.

Data Needs

Data Requirements

Utilizing the MITRE Corporation designation of P (primary), S (secondary), and T (tertiary), data elements would be classified as follows:

1 Number of court days arrest-sentencing IMPACT court (*P*—special reporting form, Prosecutor, Project Director, quarterly)*

2. Number of court days arrest—sentencing other courts (*P*—Prosecutor, Project Director, quarterly)

3. Number of first offenders processed through court, Number of second, third—offenders processed through the Court (*S*, special reporting form, prosecutor, project director, assessed semi-annually)

4. Number of offenders re-arrested before sentencing (*P*, IMPACT Case Tracking, Special Reporting form, quarterly assessment)

---

* Depends upon date of sentencing of particular case. Special reporting form cannot be submitted before then.

5. Number of target offender cases placed on bail (S, PMS, monthly)
6. Number of target offender cases detained after arraignment (S, PMS, monthly)
7. Number of target offender cases involving IMPACT program participants (S, Special Reporting Form) (Note: all three will all be gathered via special reporting form)
8. Number of target offender cases ROR after arraignment (S, PMS)
9. Number of cases reviewed by Complaint and Indictment section (S, monthly, PMS)
10. Number of cases arraigned in municipal court (S, monthly, PMS)
11. Number of cases—preliminary hearing (S, monthly, PMS)
12. Number of cases presented to Grand Jury (S, monthly, PMS)
13. Number of cases where Grand Jury sends down indictment (S, monthly, PMS)
14. Number of cases where Grand Jury dismisses (S, monthly, PMS)
15. Number of cases assigned to each IMPACT judge (S, Quarterly, Special Reporting Form)
16. Number of cases pleading "guilty" before IMPACT judge (S, Quarterly, Special Reporting Form)
17. Number of offenders × sentence alternative, guilty pleadings (Semi-annual Special reporting Form)
18. Number of months/offender sentenced after guilty pleading (Semi-annual Special Reporting Form)
19. Number of trials (jury/non-jury) held per IMPACT court (S, Monthly, PMS)
20. Number of cases decided "guilty" (S, Special Reporting Form)
21. Number of cases decided "not guilty" (S, Special Reporting Form)
22. Number of guilty offenders × sentencing alternative, number of months/offender for these sentences (Special reporting format, assessed semi-annually)
23. Number of Newark residents charged

24. Number of offenders charged by type of IMPACT crime (special reporting form, assessed semi-annually)

Data Constraints

Aside from potential problems in measuring the number of court days in other courts (non-IMPACT), there would seem to be no constraints in collecting data for this project.

Data Collection and Management

Data with respect to achievement of some performance and all capability objectives will be collected via the IMPACT PMS reporting system, attached. Monthly reporting forms, with projections for the month matched against actual achievement will be submitted to IMPACT for monitoring and analysis. When a report comes in for a particular reporting month, attached to it are the projections for the following month, and so on for twelve operating months.

Management of PMS data will rest with the IMPACT Assistant Director for Police and Courts. Data reduction and analysis will be performed jointly by the assistant director and the IMPACT Evaluation Director.

Evaluation reports (to be issued quarterly) will be submitted through the IMPACT Director jointly by the CAT Evaluation Director and the Assistant Director for Police and Courts.

Data Validation

Validity as to the reporting of project monitor data to IMPACT will be assured by on-site visits by the CAT assistant director for Police and Courts (and any assistants he has to delegate that task).

Data utilized to evaluate performance objectives flow from reliable criminal justice agencies (Police and Courts); therefore, there are no plans to audit that data.

Evaluation Analysis

The essential thrust of the evaluation analysis is to assess the amount of time it takes an offender (consistent with maintaining a specified "quality of justice" level) from arrest to sentencing. This will be assessed via an aforementioned special reporting form. Supplementary analysis will include assessing general caseload levels (by type of IMPACT crime), as well as various data dimensions, enumerated above on the type of offenders processed.

Timing

The nature of the evaluation analysis (procuring data from special reporting forms) does not permit a regular quarterly assessment for data on the time it takes an offender to be processed. (The projected time is anywhere between 60-90 days). IMPACT will not receive this special reporting form until at least a week after sentence; therefore, it can be expected that an initial assessment of time would not be made until the middle of November 1973.

IMPACT Case Tracking—An Assessment of Recidivism

IMPACT is currently attempting to establish a system to track rehabilitative offenders as to their criminal activity after release from the project. The system will operate as follows:

Information concerning each participant will be gathered via an IMPACT Participant Profile form.

This form will be completed by the project director, and filed in the project's files. In addition, light blue 3 × 5 index cards containing "condensed" tracking information for each offender will be completed by the applicant (from the IMPACT Participant Profile form) and filed in alphabetical order by last name in the Newark Police Department criminal history file. These cards are numbered consecutively and as such each particpant is identified by his own number (called an "IMPACT Circular Number"). When an arrest report is filed, NPD personnel must check the criminal history file (as a matter of course) and if the arrest report matches the IMPACT offender, a special report attached here will be filed to the IMPACT office. (Note: The special report will be mailed to IMPACT on a

LEVEL 1: Explanation of Project Monitor-Quantified.			
Special Case Processing PROJECT: for IMPACT Offenders	COMPONENT:	GEOGRAPHIC AREA: Newark	DATE:
1. Project or Component Object	Project Objective Description		
	Performance Objectives		
FIRST	To complete the adjudication process from arrest to sentencing for Newark offenders charged with IMPACT crimes within 90 days and as close to 60 days as possible (45% reduction).		
SECOND	To achieve collateral benefits throughout the Newark-Essex Courts System, reducing overall delays by 10%.		
THIRD	To achieve crime prevention benefits from the court process by arriving at a judicial determination in close proximity to the commission of a crime thereby reducing the amount of re-arrests prior to sentencing.		
FOURTH	To improve the overall quality of justice.		
FIFTH	Capability Objectives		
	To provide the municipal court the resources and supportive personnel necessary to rapidly process and refer complaints involving IMPACT crimes.		
SIXTH	To provide the county courts the resources and supportive personnel necessary to complete the adjudication process through sentencing within 90 days.		
SEVENTH			
EIGHTH			

FIGURE VII-3. Impact Performance Management System.

daily basis regardless of whether an arrest occurs. This is to assure data accuracy).

For the Court Program care must be taken not to complete a participant profile and a 3 × 5 index card (and therefore assign a name) to a previous offender participating in an IMPACT program. (He or she will have a participant profile and a number already assigned).

The purpose here is to avoid duplication of numbers. "Recidivism" data will be aggregated on a monthly basis. To assure confidentiality, only the NPD and the project will have an awareness of who was arrested; IMPACT will possess only numbers and a master reference form indicating to which project that number belongs.

REFERENCES

Adams, Stuary, *Evaluate Research in Corrections: A Practical Guide*, Law Enforcement Assistance Administration, Washington D.C.: U. S. Government Printing Office, March, 1975. One of Law Enforcement Assistance Administration's prescriptive packages in evaluation. Discusses role of agency administrators, research methods and provides six case studies of evaluative research impact.

Carter, Robert, "The Evaluation of Police Programs," *The Police Chief*, November, 1971. Provides an overview of factors to utilize in evaluating programs. Concepts are particularly useful in helping to design an evaluation component.

Evaluation in Criminal Justice Programs: Guidelines and Examples, The Mitre Corporation, National Impact Program Evaluation, Law Enforcement Assistance Administration, Washington, D.C.: U. S. Government Printing Office, May, 1973. A step by step "How To" approach for conducting evaluations. Provides examples for a variety of criminal justice projects. *High Impact Anti-Crime Program*, U. S. Department of Justice, Law Enforcement Assistance Administration, Superintendant of Documents, Washington, D. C.: Government Printing Office, July, 1974. Presents evaluation designs for Law Enforcement Assistance Administration high impact funding program. Evaluation examples are given for corrections, courts and police.

Suchman, Edward, *Evaluative Research*, New York, Russell Sage Foundation, 1967. One of the classic approaches to evaluative research. Highly academic in the approach to evaluation.

Chapter Objectives

1. Defends the person who is responsible for planning.
2. Illustrates the impact that the chief executive attitude toward planning has on an agency's planning process.
3. Discusses the problems standing in the way of the chief executive's discharge of planning responsibilities.
4. Indicates the considerations in developing the planning organization.
5. Illustrates different planning structures currently in use.
6. Discusses the relationships of the planning organization with the other departments in an agency.
7. Considers the question of whether an agency should have a planning organization.
8. Discusses the pitfalls and mistakes which typically occur in operation of the planning process.

8
Organization and Pitfalls of Planning

An important responsibility of top management in all but the very smallest criminal justice agency is to organize planning within the agency. Because all operational supervisors have planning responsibilities and most staffs also become involved in agency planning, decisions must be made about which duties should be assigned to which people, what authority each should have, and what problems the planner should anticipate. In this chapter we will discuss planning in terms of whose responsibility is it, what organization is needed for planning, and what pitfalls the planner should anticipate.

Whose Responsibility?

There can and will be no effective comprehensive criminal justice planning in any organization where the chief executive does not give it firm support and make sure that others in the organization understand the depth of commitment. This principle should be obvious; but oftentimes it is not. Even when it is accepted, the role of the chief executive is far from clear. Surveys of planning problems and personnel observations point to the fact that an insufficient commitment to planning by agency top management is far too prevalent.

These failures may grow out of a lack of understanding by top management of its responsibilities. One expert (Mace 1965, p. 50) stated:

> Probably the single most important problem in agency planning derives from the belief of some chief operating executives that agency planning is not a function with which they should

be directly concerned. They regard planning as something to be delegated, which subordinates can do without responsible participation by chief executives. They think the end result of effective planning is the compilation of a "Plans" book. Such volumes get distributed to key executives, who scan the contents briefly, file them away, breathe a sigh of relief, and observe. Thank goodness that is done—now let's get back to work.

On the other hand there are many agency heads—but obviously not enough of them—who fully comprehend the primacy of their responsibilities for planning. It is clear that the job of planning and keeping the organization moving toward its goal is the task of the agency head. This position, alone, can serve as 'ringmaster' in keeping all the diverse efforts and operations of the organization headed in the same direction. The tasks are shared in some measure and operational problems delegated, but steady hands must be on the reins at all times to ensure optimum coordination and continuity.

This is a big responsibility and a difficult one. It means that the chief executive must keep abreast of broad economic, social, political, and scientific trends and developments outside the immediate agency that may at a future point have great impacts on this agency.

But even when a chief executive accepts the importance of the role in planning it is not always easy to find the time to do what is required with confidence, or to determine precisely what ones role ought to be in the many activities, and with the many individuals and groups concerned with planning. There is no single way to discharge properly the many responsibilities in planning. The issues are subtle, complex, and vary much from one agency to another, from one man to another, and over time.

Time, Temperament, and Dilemmas

Major problems standing in the way of many chief executives' clarification and discharge of their planning role are the shortage of time, lack of proper temperament, and difficulties in resolving the many dilemmas they face. These problems deserve some attention.

One of the paradoxes of modern corporate life is that while increased mechanization has eased the physical burden of work and the average work week has shortened, the burdens and work week of the typical supervisor have expanded. A major reason for the heavier executive load is that complications in management increase at a faster rate than the development and application of tools and techniques to lighten the tasks.

Most chief executives rise to the top of their companies through one or several functional areas. Depending upon the individual, of course, this may not only give a bias in favor of self experience, but may also find old patterns of thinking uncongenial to the requirements of overall corporate planning. A person who has spent their life in line-action may find uncomfortable the type of thinking required in comprehensive planning. The crux of the matter is that the behavioral requirements of planning as a management task are often different from, or in conflict with, the processes and content of management work normally prevalent in the organization.

It is easy to see how a person who has been concerned with acting decisively on short-range problems and has never really set about formulating broad long-range plans can, upon reaching the chief executive office, fully accept the responsibility for corporate planning but never really fully discharge the task. Personal temperament may not be well-suited to the planning job and this may be reinforced by a lack of experience in doing it.

Lack of experience with, or unease in conducting, corporate planning should not be an excuse for neglecting the job. There are ways to overcome this problem, not the least of which is to share the work with another line officer, or a staff-man, who has the proper credentials and motivation to complement the personality and interests of the chief executive.

Built into chief executive jobs are many dilemmas that can be barriers to asserting strong leadership and participation in planning. On the one hand the chief executive must guarantee a reasonable degree of stability and routine in his business. An agency cannot long endure if standard procedures are absent and instability upsets equanimity. On the other hand, the chief executive must be either the architect or major innovator of change. At the extreme, each of these forces inhibits the other. There are ways to find out what is happening and to control events without inhibiting the initiative of people. One outstanding method is to step up to the job of designing and maintaining an effective agency planning and control system.

Of first importance is the fact that for criminal justice agency planning to be successful the chief executive must "buy" the idea. More than 'lip service' must give the effort. A proper planning climate is essential for effective planning. Best results are achieved when this begins with top management —the very top. They must buy the proposition that planning per se is an identifiable, controllable function essential to the health of the agency. And top management will be completely convinced only if it does a little work on the subject.

Effective planning requires involvement by the chief executive in particular, and top management generally. This in turn will stimulate involvement of all supervisors throughout an organization. Unfortunately there is no simple answer to the question: how shall the chief executive participate in planning? It has been emphasized that (Steiner, 1969, p.95):

> For the first planning effort the chief executive must be deeply involved. As experience is acquired and more staff help is available, a chief executive will know better where and when to become involved in order to exert his proper influence. The degree of involvement also will be influenced by the style of the chief executive, whether he is a 'loner' or a democratic-participative operator. Much will depend upon the size of an enterprise, its problems, personalities, and types of industry.

The chief executive must not become too involved in planning. If so, other duties will be neglected and frustrations will sour the individual on planning. Only the chief executive can determine where the correct balance lies between proper and excessive participation in an agency's planning process.

Planning done with and on behalf of top management should result in operating decisions. Without decisions the planning process is incomplete. Failure to take action on prepared plans, or continuous vacillation, will weaken staff efforts. People simply will not be motivated to exert the energy, develop the creativity and use the imagination needed to make quality plans if top management ignores them or cannot seem to act upon them.

This of course does not mean a blind devotion to a plan. Depending upon circumstances, it may be wise for a manager to make decisions that are different from those planned. Plans ought to be implemented with flexibility. Chief executives have a responsibility to see that decisions are made in light of plans and evolving circumstances—not blindly, not without reference to plans, but related meaningfully within a planning framework.

Organization for Planning

It is the major responsibility of the chief executive to see that the proper agency planning system is developed and maintained. In this effort, of course, help from subordinates will come from both line supervisors and staffs. But this individual has the responsibility to make sure that the system is appropriate to the agency and that it is done at a cost (using this word broadly) benefit.

Considering the size of the agency is a major consideration. In a very small criminal justice agency the chief executive has no choice but to do all the planning. As an agency grows, use may be made of immediate line officers to help do the planning. In larger organizations the decision may be made to establish a separate staff to help with organizational planning. If a staff is created, the chief executive must see that it begins with the proper sponsorship.

This is not meant to imply that chief executives must get enmeshed in all the grubby details of a total planning program. What is being said is that the chief must see to it that the job of planning the plan is done, that authority is clear, and that the process is put into operation.

It is very important that the chief executive name a staff director of planning (if there is one) who will reflect this determination to have an effective planning program. Or, if authority for helping to lead and do the planning job is given to a functional or line supervisor, the assignment ought to be made to a person who commands the respect of the organization. If, for example, a person is made director of planning in order to effect removal from line job failure or if the job is filled in such a way that people calculate it to be a demotion, or if a weak and obscure person is given the task, the probability of success is not favorable. If, on the other hand, the planning director is obviously well qualified, well suited for the job, and is given the fullest support by top management, success is much more likely. The same comments apply to a functional officer or an assistant to the chief executive, who might be assigned duties concerned with planning.

There are many ways to split planning responsibilities. Whatever they are, the chief executive should at least establish the pattern desired and at most should make sure the system is understood and that the responsibility of each manager is reasonably clear.

Organization for planning is very important, but as one expert says (Seymour Tilles, 1964):

> The formal distribution of planning responsibility is less significant than the degree to which the top executives of the company, and especially the chief executive, see themselves as significant contributors to the planning process.

There is no single organizational planning pattern that fits all agencies nor is there a single best organization for planning. Factors influencing planning organization vary much among agencies, but there are planning arrangements that are becoming more frequently employed.

Examination of both local and state agencies reveals that there are five basic classifications of formal planning organization. From the simplest to the most elaborate they are as follows:

1. No formal planning exists at all. Planning is done, but it is a part of the duty of each executive and no effort is made to formalize the process. This pattern is typical of many very small agencies with few managers.
2. Organized planning is done within a functional activ-

ity. The area can be administrative, operations or finance. For example, planning in a police system may center in the patrol division because crime evaluation is a function about which organized planning for such agencies may be developed.

3. A planning executive and organization may exist in the divisions of an agency or operating units in the field, but no planning staff exists at the central level. In such cases the chief executive may serve as a central focal point for planning, aided by functional officers from headquarters.

4. A central headquarters planning department is created but no planning executives or staffs are established in operating units. In such instances, of course, the planning department usually gets involved in detailed planning.

5. A planning executive and staff exists at the central headquarters and in each major division or operating unit.

Relationships

One of the most frequent and important misunderstandings of the planning process that have been found among some chief executives concerns their relationships with their planning staffs. When a chief executive uses line officers as staff to help with planning, or hires an assistant aid, or creates a planning staff, the chief is merely extending the capabilities of the office. These people are helping accomplish this one job. This is a recognition that the world is too large for one person to grasp completely and that if others can help, the chief will be more capable of examining a wider range of threats to and opportunities for the organization.

Although problems arise in defining the relationship between the chief executive and any one person, group, or other assisting organization, the most complex issues exist between the chief executive and planning staff. Clarification of roles of participants in the process is important, and a major responsibility for clarification rests with the chief executive.

A staff cannot and should not be asked to make plans for an agency. That is clearly a line job. Staffs assist line supervisors in making plans.

Even though all levels of management participate in making plans, a chief executive cannot delegate the assignment and wait until someone hands over the completed plans. If the job of making plans is delegated to a planning staff, the chief may be left in an untenable position. On the one hand, if many changes are made, a substantial redoing of plans may be automatically forced. This is expensive and unlikely to produce the sort of staff enthusiasm the best planning requires. On the other hand, if few or no changes are made, there is a danger of being a captive of the staff.

Furthermore, if the latter course is taken, the responsibilities of guiding and directing the agency's forward movement has not been discharged, even though there is staff agreement. The most important consequence of this, if continued, is a deterioration of planning capability. The most useable end product of planning is not a paper, but a person thoroughly immersed in the subject—a person whose mind is trained to act, having taken everything into account, on the spur of the moment. And that is why the ultimate decision-maker must actively participate in the planning exercise.

Relationships with line and staff people are also influenced by styles of management. A strong one-man executive may specify long-range objectives and give them to staff and line managers in the form of an edict. This is not likely to produce the desired results, but it may. Problems can be predicted if a strong executive has objectives, but, for personal reasons, is unwilling to phrase them. This leaves both line and staff with wind but without rudder. A better relationship would be one where setting agency objectives is a continuous process of the intermingling of top management views, staff recommendations, top management approval and suggestion, new staff work, new approval, and so on.

The relationships between the chief executive and the planning staff encounter many subtle human relations issues that are complicated by the special problems of planning. For example, there is a most sensitive question which arises between a planner and the chief executive with respect to frank and open discussion. The chief executive has the most prestigious position in the agency and may frequently act imperiously—freely imposing one's will whenever desirable.

The staff planner, in helping the chief executive with the job, feels (rightfully) the enormous significance of accomplished activities. Yet its inappropriate to speak as freely as if they are on the same level. The best assurance that each is contributing the maximum to the planning effort is the development of a mutual respect and confidence. This is a two-way street, requiring appropriate efforts on the part of both.

Should an Agency Have a Planning Department?

Planning departments are expensive and not without problems. An important question arises, therefore, concerning the desirability of having such departments.

In a larger agency, a separate planning department has many advantages. Any department that can suitably discharge the functions sketched above for a planning group will clearly fill a major need in a larger agency. A planning department should be able to fulfill these duties with objective judgment and the application of the latest problem-solving tools. In this fashion, functional biases are submerged and staff work is up-to-date.

If a planning staff becomes removed from operations or tries to do all the planning, it should not be allowed to exist. If it becomes abstract and abstruse in its thinking and deals in matters unrelated to management problems, it should and will be eliminated.

If the existence of a planning department is used as an excuse for top management to avoid responsibilities for corporate planning, the department should not have been created in the first place.

Pitfalls in Planning

Up to this point many of the positive attributes of planning have been discussed and have overlooked some of the pitfalls that planners fall into as they go through their planning process. The remainder of this chapter will be dedicated to a brief description of potential planning problem areas.

Gathering Excessive Data

As planners begin to perform their job, they typically become obsessed with the need for more data. They tend to look at data in terms of absoluteness, that is—they are looking to describe something from data in a finite form. Actually, the converse is true, data should be used as an indicator of change or rate of change. We are not so concerned that a given jurisdiction had 25 homicides as we are with knowing if homicides are increasing or decreasing and at what rate.

The planner should select in advance the minimal data needed to make a decision with 70 to 80 percent certainty. The planner must select data sources carefully in order to identify the most useful and pertinent. A good "rule of thumb" to consider is that 80 to 90 percent of planning can be accomplished with data that is readily available, thus requiring only 10 percent of the planning resources to assimilate. In order to get the remaining 10 to 20 percent will require an investment of almost 90 percent of your planning resources. Capturing original data is a time consuming and expensive proposition and should be considered only after all other readily available sources of data have been explored.

Misinterpretation of Data

In reviewing and analyzing data, keep the problem in mind and be sure that the data applies. It is so easy to "lose sight of the forest because of the trees." If uncertainty arises as to the meaningfulness of the data, do not be afraid to seek the opinion and judgment of others who are knowledgeable. Agency heads or supervisors are a great help in interpreting data once it has been separated into a digestible format.

Inadequate Definition of the Problem

As the planner defines the problem, the limits or boundaries of the problem description must also be defined. By doing this, the planner will set a finite number of factors influencing the problem that can reasonably be addressed. If the boundaries are not defined, a chain reaction of seemingly endless problem area influences will occur. As one influence is identified, factors impeding the influence will be discovered and so on until the planner will become so lost in the trivia of cause and effect that one could forget or lose sight of the initial problem. Again, advice from appropriate and knowledgeable criminal justice agency personnel can be an asset in establishing problem area boundaries.

Lack of Understanding of the Criminal Justice System

The planner tends to overly simplify the workings of the criminal justice system. One reason—an incomplete awareness of the day-to-day operations, procedures, technicalities and internal influences of the system. This calls for recognizing this handicap and seeking input from people and literature which expresses these problem and solution impeding influences.

Establishment of Irrelevant Objectives

As was stated earlier, all objectives should be quantified and bound by a time constraint. Additionally, they must be related to the accomplishment of a specific goal. All objectives tend to get compromised as policy makers realize that they are committing themselves to a specific output over a given time. In order to protect the goal maker from potential failure they will reword objectives into a less specific format. This threat will represent a constant challenge to planners and evaluators for many years to come.

Premature Acceptance of a Plan Without Considering Alternatives

As long as criminal justice planning is tied to the chariot of federal funding, the planner is going to be placed in the position of finding problems to fit desired solutions. The planner must make an effort to expose policy people to the fact that more than one solution approach is possible and that sufficient considerations should be given to the feasibility consideration discussed in a previous chapter.

Improper Allocation of Solution Resources

The planning process spends considerable time toward the prioritization of problem, goals and solutions just to find that resources to solve the problem are distributed haphazardly between both high and low priority areas. Work on the most critical problems first. Allocate resources in proportion to the importance of the problem giving proper attention to critical problems. Policy makers should be encouraged to allocate sufficient funds to each project to assure that it can obtain its stated objectives.

Lack of Criteria for Appraisal

Solution oriented projects and tasks should be monitored frequently based upon performance standards for appraising progress. The whole purpose of this is not to penalize someone for doing a poor job but rather to take timely corrective action when needed.

Insufficient Emphasis on Planning Organization

As a planning activity begins to take hold in an organization the planning unit becomes saddled with a multitude of duties and activities simply because it has available manpower and no one else seems to be appropriate for the job. Many times this is a result of the planner wanting to be accepted in an organization so the planning group deals with almost any request that is funneled in its direction. This is a good idea during the formation period of the planning group. It helps them integrate into the organization. However, the planner must be aware of a primary mission—and that is planning. It is imperative to focus efforts on planning and minimize other duties, also being cautious to assign or assume planning responsibilities in proportion to staff size and workload.

Lack of Coordination with Other Activities

One of the major activities of planning is coordination. If the planner does not coordinate, nobody else will. The planner should identify the universe of problems related to certain efforts at state, regional, local and departmental levels. After ascertaining relationships with other agency efforts, a working relationship with the planning staffs of these organizational units can be established.

These are but a few of the pitfalls that will confront a planner during operations on a daily basis. Many more problems will obviously be encountered. The key to success is to not loose sight of the planning objective, even if this means compromising a smaller portion of it to gain the greater portion.

Summary

This chapter has emphasized that the chief executive of a criminal justice agency has the ultimate responsibility for planning. However, the discharge of this responsibility is more often than not watered down by the executive's inability to find sufficient time for planning, an unfamiliarity with the planning process, or fear of participation in the planning function. The organization required for planning is dependent upon the size of the criminal justice system agency and its particular needs. In many cases there may not be sufficient justification for a special staff of planners, rather the responsibility will be shared by the chief executive and an operational managerial staff. In any case there is always a need to plan; and planning, to be effective in an agency, must involve top management staff and operational personnel commitment and input.

The wise planner should, from the beginning, be sensitive to some pitfalls in planning that are almost sure to be experienced. They include:

- Gathering excessive data.
- Misinterpretating data.
- Inadequate definition of the problem.
- Establishment of irrelevant objectives.
- Lack of understanding of the criminal justice system.
- Premature acceptance of a plan without considering alternatives.
- Improper allocation of solution resources.
- Lack of criteria for appraisal.

- Insufficient emphasis on planning organization and, lastly
- Lack of coordination with other activities.

Topics for Discussion

1. Discuss the role of the chief executive in the planning process.

2. Describe how the chief executive's temperament affects the acceptance of planning.

3. Discuss the relationship of a chief executive to his planning department.

4. Discuss how to organize for planning.

5. Discuss the relationship of a planning department to the line and staff.

6. Discuss the lack of understanding of the criminal justice system as a pitfall to planning.

REFERENCES

Albanese, Robert, *Management: Toward Accountability for Performance*, Homewood, Illinois: Richard Irwin, 1975. A general text in management, selected chapters cover managerial responsibilities in the planning process.

Haimann, Theo, and William Scott, *Management in the Modern Organization*, Boston: Houghton Mifflin Co., 1974. Discusses the management functions of planning in detail. Has several case studies in planning relative to business organizations.

Mace, Myles L., "The President and Corporate Planning," *Harvard Business Review*, January-February, 1965. This is an article on the role of the top executive with respect to planning within his organization. Covers pitfalls and suggests procedural recommendations.

Steiner, George A., *Top Management Planning*, London: The McMillan Company, 1969. Focusing on the problems top managers encounter in developing, maintaining and improving planning systems, this text offers comprehensive analyses of every aspect of planning.

Tilles, Seymour, *Strategic Planning in the Multi-Divisional Company,*
Boston: Boston Safe Deposit and Trust Company, 1964. (Mul-
tilithed) This article relates planning to large organizations.
Emphasis is on long range planning.

Chapter Objectives

1. Introduces the reader to a few examples of federal funding sources.
2. Develops a proper attitude toward preparing a grant proposal.
3. Encourages proper program development before actually writing a grant proposal.
4. Suggestions on who should write the proposal.
5. Suggestions on writer's attitude toward application forms and instructions for preparation.
6. Recommendations on how to write a grant application: a description of what most funding agencies look for in a meritorious grant application.
7. Suggestions for proof reading.

9

Grantsmanship—A Perspective

It will be assumed that if the reader has spent the time required to read all of the preceeding chapters, he probably is one or more of the following:

- A student of planning with an interest in funding.
- Practitioner interested in professionalization.
- Intent upon learning how to prepare a grant application.
- Frustrated because of earlier unrewarded attempts to prepare successful grant applications and wondering about the cause(s) of rejection.

It has been the intent of the authors of this work on criminal justice planning to provide the reader with a basic knowledge of the intricacies of planning and, in this chapter, to highlight the pitfalls, common errors and faults of the grant application process. Although grant application procedures and forms vary with funding agencies, there is a similarity of scheme common to all. Many prospective proponents are mystified by the processes involved or feel overwhelmed by the paperwork. This is not an uncommon feeling experienced by all grant applicants at one time or another. Like any stress game, however, grantmanship can be learned and played with very substantial ultimate reward. It is hoped that this section will be useful to the reader in very practical terms.

This chapter will elaborate on possible funding sources for criminal justice agency use. The resource section at the end of the chapter presents a step by step guide to grant preparation.

Funding Sources

Funding sources are available to the adventurous. Time, effort and a certain amount of frustration are the bedfellows accompanying one throughout the process. However, a funding source can be found, providing your project has merit. Local government is an appropriate and logical place to begin. Local government funds numerous community oriented projects as well as those originating through agencies of the system. It's important, however to understand the nature of local political jurisdiction in order to assess the chances for success. If project implementation cannot wait until an unfavorable local government political climate changes, other sources must be sought. A note of caution, though, many funding sources that might be available will require local governmental support.

A possible funding source accessible to the criminal justice system is the *Law Enforcement Assistance Administration (LEAA)*. Funding is made available through national, state and regional levels. Basically, there are four types of funding sources provided through LEAA. Utilization of LEAA funds requires local government support.

Part B Funds

Part B funds are exclusively used for planning grants—these are provided to state planning agencies or regional planning agencies for the purpose of developing law enforcement and criminal justice plans based on their evaluation of state and local problems in this area. Regional planning agencies are comprised of local units of government often joined together by a joint powers agreement or some other arrangement which legally establishes the planning authority. These regional planning agencies should be contacted and utilized as a valuable resource in securing funds and for project development.

Part C Funds

Part C funds are available to criminal justice and private agencies and provide an excellent funding source. As stated in the Crime Control Act of 1973, the purpose of Part C funds is to encourage states and units of general local government to carry out programs and projects to improve and strengthen law enforcement and criminal justice. LEAA is authorized to make grants under this part for:

(1) Public protection, including the development, demonstration, evaluation, implementation, and purchase of methods, devices, facilities, and equipment designed to improve and strengthen law enforcement and criminal justice and reduce crime in public and private places.

(2) The recruiting of law enforcement and criminal justice personnel and the training of personnel in law enforcement and criminal justice.

(3) Public education relating to crime prevention and encouraging respect for law and order, including education programs in schools and programs to improve public understanding of and cooperation with law enforcement and criminal justice agencies.

(4) Constructing building or other physical facilities which would fulfill or implement the purpose of this section, including local correctional facilities, centers for the treatment of narcotic addicts, and temporary courtroom facilities in areas of high crime incidence.

(5) The organization, education, and training of special law enforcement and criminal justice units to combat organized crime, including the establishment and development of state organized crime prevention councils, the recruiting and training of special investigative and prosecuting personnel, and the development of systems for collecting, storing, and disseminating information relating to the control of organized crime.

(6) The organization, education, and training of regular law enforcement and criminal justice units, and law enforcement reserve units for the prevention, detection, and control of riots and other violent civil disorders, including the acquisition of riot control equipment.

(7) The recruiting, organization, training, and education of community service officers to serve with and assist local and state law enforcement and criminal justice agencies in the discharge of their duties through such activities as recruiting; improvement of police-community relations and grievance resolution mechanisms; community patrol activities; encouragement of neighborhood participation in crime prevention and public safety efforts; and other activities designed to improve police capabilities, public safety and the objectives of this section: Provided. That in no case shall a grant be made under this subcategory without the approval of the local government or local law enforcement and criminal justice agency.

(8) The establishment of a Criminal Justice Coordinating Council for any unit of general local government or any combination of such units within the state, having a population of two hundred and fifty thousand or more, to assure improved planning and coordination of all law enforcement and criminal justice activities.

(9) The development and operation of community-based delinquent prevention and correctional programs, emphasizing halfway houses and other community-based rehabilitation centers for initial preconviction or post-conviction referral of offenders; expanded probationary programs, including paraprofessional and volunteer participation; and community service centers for the guidance and supervision of potential repeat youthful offenders.

(10) The establishment of interstate metropolitan regional planning units to prepare and coordinate plans of state and local governments and agencies concerned with regional planning for metropolitan areas.

Part D Funds

Under Part D (Sec. 402) of the Crime Control Act of 1973 the National Institute of Law Enforcement and Criminal Justice was established. It is the purpose of the Institute to encourage research and development to improve and strengthen law enforcement and criminal justice, to disseminate the results of such efforts to state and local government, and to assist in the development and support of programs for the training of law enforcement and criminal justice personnel.

The Institute is authorized—

(1) to make grants to, or enter into contracts with, public agencies, institutions of higher education, or private organizations to conduct research, demonstrations, or special projects pertaining to the purposes described in this title, including the development of new or improved approaches, techniques, systems, equipment, and devices to improve and strengthen law enforcement and criminal justice;

(2) to make continuing studies and undertake programs of research to develop new or improved approaches, techniques, systems, equipment, and devices to improve and strengthen law enforcement and criminal justice, including, but not limited to, the effectiveness of projects or programs carried out under this title;

(3) to carry out programs of behavioral research designed to provide more accurate information on the causes of crime and the effectiveness of various means of preventing crime, and to evaluate the success of correctional procedures;

(4) to make recommendations for action which can be taken by federal, state, and local governments and by private persons and organizations to improve and strengthen law enforcement and criminal justice;

(5) to carry out programs of instructional assistance consisting of research fellowships for the programs provided under this section, and special workshops for the presentation and dissemination of information resulting from research, demonstrations, and special projects authorized by this title:

(6) to assist in conducting, at the request of a state or a unit of general local government or a combination thereof, local or regional training programs for the training of state and local law enforcement and criminal justice personnel, including but not limited to those engaged in the investigation of crime and apprehension of criminals, community relations, the prosecution or defense of those charged with crime, corrections, rehabilitation, probation and parole of offenders. Such training activities shall be designed to supplement and improve rather than supplant the training activities of the state and units of general local government and shall not duplicate the training activities of the Federal Bureau of Investigation under section 404 of this title. While participating in the training program or traveling in connection with participation in the training program, state and local personnel shall be allowed travel expenses and a per diem allowance in the same manner as prescribed under section 5703 (b) of title 5, United States Code, for persons employed intermittently in the Government service;

(7) to carry out a program of collection and dissemination of information obtained by the Institute or other federal agencies, public agencies, institutions of higher education, or private organizations engaged in projects under this title, including information relating to new or improved approaches, techniques, systems, equipment, and devices to improve and strengthen law enforcement: and

(8) to establish a research center to carry out the programs described in this section.

Part E Funds

Part E funds are designated for use in the area of corrections, including facilities and programs. These monies are usually allocated to the State Planning Agencies for dispersal to Regional Planning Agencies based on competitive need. LEAA is authorized to make a grant under this part to a State Planning Agency if the application incorporated in the State Plan:

(1) sets forth a comprehensive statewide program for the construction, acquisition, or renovation of correctional institutions and facilities in the State and the improvement of correctional programs and practices throughout the state;

(2) provides satisfactory assurances that the control of the funds and title to property derived therefrom shall be in a public agency for the uses and purposes provided in this part and that a public agency will administer those funds and that property;

(3) provides satisfactory assurances that the availability of funds under this part shall not reduce the amount of funds under part C of this title which a state would, in the absence of funds under this part, allocate for purposes of this part;

(4) provides satisfactory emphasis on the development and operation of community-based correctional facilities and programs, including diagnostic services, halfway houses, probation, and other supervisory release programs for preadjudication and postadjudication referral of delinquents, youthful offenders, the first offenders and community-oriented programs for the supervision of parolees;

(5) provides for advanced techniques in the design of institutions and facilities;

(6) provides where feasible and desirable, for the sharing of correctional institutions and facilities on a regional basis;

(7) provides satisfactory assurances that the personnel standards and programs of the institutions and facilities will reflect advanced practices;

(8) provides satisfactory assurances that the state is engaging in projects and programs to improve the recruiting, organization, training, and education of personnel employed in correctional activities, including those of probation, parole, and rehabilitation;

(9) provides necessary arrangements for the development and operation of narcotic and alcoholism treatment programs in correctional institutions and facilities and in connection with probation or other supervisory release programs for all persons, incarcerated or on parole, who are drug addicts, drug abusers, alcoholics, or alcohol abusers;

(10) complies with the same requirements established for comprehensive state plans under paragraphs (1), (3), (5), (6), (8), (9), (10), (11), (12), (13), (14), and (15) of section 303 (a) of this title;

(11) provides for accurate and complete monitoring of the progress and improvement of the correctional system. Such monitoring shall include rate of prisoner rehabilitation and rates of recidivism in comparison with previous performance of the state or local correctional systems and current performance of other state and local prison systems not included in this program; and

(12) provides that state and local governments shall submit such annual reports as the Administrator may require.

Juvenile Justice and Delinquency Prevention Act of 1974

The Juvenile Justice and Delinquency Prevention Act was signed by President Gerald R. Ford on September 7, 1974. Its importance was reemphasized in the May/June, 1975 issue of Soundings:

> The provisions of the Act are significant. It establishes an Office of Juvenile Justice and Delinquency Prevention in the Department of Justice's Law Enforcement Assistance Administration (LEAA) to coordinate all federal juvenile justice programs; sets up a National Advisory Committee on Juvenile Justice and Delinquency Prevention to advise the LEAA on federal juvenile delinquency programs; provides block grants to state and local governments and grants to public and private agencies to develop juvenile justice programs with special emphasis on the prevention of delinquency; and creates a National Institute for Juvenile Justice and Delinquency Prevention to serve as a clearinghouse for delinquency information and to conduct training, research, demonstrations and evaluation of juvenile justice programs.

Participation in the Act, however, by any state is voluntary.

> The requirements in the Act regarding distribution of the funds is especially significant for community-based programs. As resources become available, formula grants will be made to the participating states on the basis of the relative population in each state under age 18. Two-thirds of the formula grants are to be expended through local units of government. Seventy-five percent of the formula grants to each state, whether expended directly by the state, or by a local unit of government, or through contracts with public or private agencies: "(Section 223, (a) (10) shall be used for advanced techniques in develop-

ing, maintaining and expanding programs and services designed to prevent juvenile delinquency, to divert juveniles from the juvenile justice system, and to provide community-based alternatives to juvenile detention and correctional facilities." Among the many programs included in the definition of advanced techniques in the Act are community-based programs and services for the prevention and treatment of juvenile delinquency including youth service bureaus, diversion programs, youth initiated programs, alternative learning situations which encourage youth to remain in school, and programs to maintain and strengthen the family unit. In addition to the above, the Act requires that at least 20 percent of the funds available for special emphasis grants shall be available to private nonprofit agencies, organizations, or institutions who have had experience in working with youth.

Initially states are encouraged to center their first plans around two actions required by the Juvenile Act. These are separation of juveniles from adults during incarceration and deinstitutionalization of status offenders.

U. S. Department of Health, Education and Welfare

Another excellent funding source is the Alcohol, Drug Abuse, and Mental Health Administration, Public Health Service, U. S. Department of Health, Education, and Welfare. Listed below are examples of some of the types of programs available. All can be found in the Catelog of Federal Domestic Assistance, published annually by the Executive Office of the President, Office of Management and Budget:

1. *13.235 Drug Abuse Community Service Programs Federal Agency:* Alcohol, Drug Abuse, and Mental Health Administration, Department of Health, Education, and Welfare.
   Objectives: To reach, treat and rehabilitate narcotic addicts, drug abusers, and drug dependent persons through a wide range of community based services by the provision of partial support of professional and technical personnel to staff community-based aftercare services. *Eligibility Requirements:*

Applicant Eligibility: For a staffing grant, applicant must be (1) a Community Mental Health Center or an affiliate of a Community Health Center; (2) a public or private nonprofit agency or organization located in an area which does not have a Community Mental Health Center. The applicant under (2) must agree to utilize existing community resources and to apply for affiliation with any future Community Mental Health Center servicing the area. Applicant must provide at least five essential services to narcotic addicts and drug dependent persons: Inpatient, outpatient, intermediate (halfway house, partial hospitalization), 24-hour emergency services, and Community-Wide consultation and education services. Applicants for drug abuse services projects must be public or private nonprofit organizations.

Beneficiary Eligibility: Narcotic addicts and drug dependent persons. A narcotic addict is any person whose use of narcotic drug causes physical, psychological, or social harm to himself or endangers the health, safety, or welfare of others. A drug dependent person is any person who uses a controlled substance and who is in a state of psychic or physical dependence, or both.

Credentials/Documentation: Proof of nonprofit status, if a private, nonprofit agency or organization. Cost will be determined in accordance with General Services Administration FMC 74-4.

Information Contacts:

Regional or Local Office: The headquarters office (National Institute on Drug Abuse) is responsible for the administration of these grant and contract community service programs.

Headquarters Office: National Instute on Alcohol, Drug Abuse, and Mental Health Administration, 11400 Rockville Pike, MD 20852 Telephone: (301) 443-6480.

2. *13.239 Narcotic Addict Rehabilitation Act–Contracts (NARA)*

Federal Agency: Alcohol, Drug Abuse, and Mental Health Administration, Public Health Service, Department of Health, Education, and Welfare

Objectives: To provide for civil commitment of narcotic addicts for examination and treatment, and for rehabilitation and after-care services for addicts.

Eligibility Requirements:

Applicant Eligibility: Individuals eligible for commitment are: (a) narcotic addicts charged with certain federal offenses who wish to be committed for treatment in lieu of prosecution (Title I); (b) narcotic addicts convicted of a federal crime who are sentenced by the court to commitment for treatment (TITLE II); (c) narcotic addicts not charged with a criminal offense who apply for commitment to treatment themselves, or for whom petition for committment is made by a related individual (Title III). *Beneficiary Eligibility:* Same as applicant eligibility.

Credentials/Documentation: Cost will be determined in accordance with General Services Administration FMC 74-4. *Information Contacts:*

Regional or Local Office: Not applicable. Headquarters Office: Director, National Institute on Drug Abuse, Alcohol, Drug Abuse, and Mental Health Administration, 11400 Rockville Pike, Rockville, MD 20852. Telephone (301) 443-6480.

3. *13.243 Alcohol, Drug Abuse, and Mental Health Administration Scientific Communications and Public Education*

   Federal Agency: Alcohol, Drug Abuse, and Mental Health Administration, Public Health Service, Department of Health, Education and Welfare

   Objectives: To provide fullest possible dissemination of alcohol, drug abuse and mental health information through full-scale program of scientific communications and public information and education activities serving both the professional community and the general public.

   Eligibility Requirements:

   Applicant Eligibility: All activities and materials are for the use and benefit of the total public.

Beneficiary Eligibility: Same as applicant eligibility.

Credentials/Documentation: costs will be determined in accordance with General Services Administration FMC 74-4.

Information Contacts:

Regional or Local Office: Not applicable.

Headquarters Office: Director, Office of Public Affairs, Alcohol, Drug Abuse, and Mental Health Administration, 5600 Fishers Lane, Rockville, MD 20852. Telephone: (301) 443-3783.

. *13.251 Alcohol Community Service Programs Federal Agency:* Alcohol, Drug Abuse, and Mental Health Administration, Public Health Service, Department of Health, Education and Welfare.

Objectives: To prevent and control alcoholism through a community based program of comprehensive services under proper medical auspices on a coordinated basis, integrated with and involving the active participation of a wide range of public and nongovernmental agencies.

Eligibility Requirements:

Applicant Eligibility: The applicant must be a community mental health center; or be a public or private nonprofit organization affiliated with a community mental health center; or be a public or private nonprofit organization located in an area which has no community mental health center which will agree to both appropriately utilize existing community resources and to apply within a reasonable time for affiliation with any future community mental health center servicing the area.

Beneficiary Eligibility: Comprehensive services must be available to all alcoholics and problem drinkers and their families who reside in the specified geographic area.

Credentials/Documentation: Proof of nonprofit status. Costs will be determined in accordance with General Services Administration FMC 74-4.

Information Contacts:

Regional or Local Office: ADAMHA Branch in the appropriate DHEW regional office.

Headquarters Office: Director, National Institute on Alcohol Abuse and Alcoholism, Alcohol, Drug Abuse, and Mental Health Administration, PHS, DHEW, 5600 Fishers Lane, Rockville, MD 20852 Telephone (301) 443-3885.

5. *13.252 Alcohol Demonstration Programs Federal Agency:* Alcohol, Drug Abuse, and Mental Health Administration, Public Health Service, Department of Health, Education, and Welfare

Objectives: To prevent and control alcoholism through development of projects relating to the provision of prevention and treatment approaches for population groups; to conduct surveys and field trials to evaluate the adequacy of programs and demonstrations of new and effective methods of delivery of services.

Eligibility Requirements:

Applicant Eligibility: The applicant for support in all cases must be public or a private nonprofit organization with expertise in the appropriate area.

Beneficiary Eligibility: Problem drinkers and their families.

Credentials/Documentation: Proof of nonprofit status. Costs will be determined in accordance with General Services Administration FMC 74-4.

Information Contacts:

Regional or Local Office: Regional Health Administrator (Alcoholism Section) of appropriate Regional Office of DHEW.

Headquarters Office: Director, National Institute on Alcohol Abuse and Alcoholism. Telephone: (301) 443-3885; Alcohol, Drug Abuse, and Mental Health Administration, PHS, DHEW, 5600 Fishers Lane, Rockville, MD 20852.

6. *13.275 Drug Abuse Education Programs* (R25) *Federal Agency:* Alcohol, Drug Abuse, and Mental Health Administration, Public Health Service, Department of Health, Education, and Welfare

Objectives: To collect, prepare and disseminate drug abuse information dealing with the use and abuse of drugs and the prevention of drug abuse.

Eligibility Requirements:

Applicant Eligibility: Applicants for drug abuse education grants must be public or private nonprofit organizations.

Beneficiary Eligibility: Narcotic addicts and drug dependent persons. A narcotic addict is any person whose use of narcotic drugs causes physical, psychological, or social harm to himself or endangers the health, safety, or welfare of others. A drug dependent person is any person who uses a controlled substance and who is in a state of psychic or physical dependence, or both.

Credentials/Documentation: Applicants for Drug Abuse Education grants must show proof of nonprofit status, if a private, nonprofit agency or organization. Cost will be determined in accordance with General Services Administration FMC 74-4.

Information Contacts:

Regional or Local Office: Not applicable.

Headquarters Office: National Institute on Drug Abuse, Alcohol, Drug Abuse, and Mental Health Administration, PHS, DHEW. 11400 Rockville Pike, Rockville, MD 20852. Telephone: (301)443-6480.

National Highway Traffic Safety Administration

Funds may be utilized through the National Highway Traffic Safety Administration for projects which involve the following:

- motor vehicle inspection
- vehicle registration
- motorcycle safety
- driver education
- driver licensing
- traffic codes and laws

- traffic courts
- alcohol in relation to highway safety
  (excluding construction and maintenance)
- traffic engineering services
- identification and surveillance of accident locations
- pedestrian and bicycle safety
- police traffic services
- debris hazzard control and cleanup
- accident investigation
- school bus safety
- community support and planning

Political subdivisions are eligible beneficiaries of these funds through your State Highway Safety Program. It would be advisable to first check with your State Department of Transportation to assure your state highway safety program is approved in accordance with uniform program area standards. These uniform program standards are available from the National Highway Traffic Safety Administration and the Federal Highway Administration.

Defense Civil Preparedness Agency

The Defense Civil Preparedness Agency provides funds to state or local (city, county, township, etc.) civil defense organizations. Funds are to be utilized in preparation against national or other emergency situations. Emergency Operation Centers are eligible for funding under this agency to provide protected facilities and communications.

Summary

This concluding chapter has acquainted the reader with a few examples of federal funding sources for criminal justice oriented project activities. These included the Law Enforcement Assistance Administration (LEAA), the Alcohol, Drug Abuse and Mental Health Administration of the U. S. Department of Health, Education and Welfare, the National Highway

Traffic Safety Administration, and the Defense Civil Preparedness Agency.

The chapter and the example in the resource section provided the reader with tips on:

- preparation of grant applications;
- the necessity for good program conceptualization and development before writing a grant application;
- who should write the application;
- how the writer should view the application forms and instructions; and,
- proofreading the completed application.

The essential emphasis of the resource section of the chapter is on "buypoints" that must be stressed in a good application. Obviously, not all of the "buypoints" will be applicable to every type of grant application, but for the most part they can and should be followed.

Topics for Discussion

1. Discuss the importance of proper program development prior to writing the grant application.
2. Briefly describe the process utilized in defining a problem.
3. Discuss the measureability of project objectives.
4. Discuss the method used in developing an evaluation component.
5. Discuss the problems of preparing a good budget.

RESOURCE

APPLICATION PREPARATION

Read And Think Before Writing

Be sure that the proposed project is consistent with the *Act* and with appropriate state and regional plans.

Read the entire set of application forms and all instructions from start to finish. Obtain answers to questions before becoming bewildered while actually completing the forms.

Get the basic proposal, all supporting data, and any other program materials together in a three-ring binder, and keep them there. Sheer disorganization is the biggest cause of headaches in preparing grant applications, and it wastes a lot of time.

The Applicant As A Salesman With A First Rate Product To Sell

Since the project application is a most important sales tool, prepare to be persuasive. Stimulate interest, capture attention, and gain support. Present the project concept in such a manner as to *excite* the reader about the idea, and make the potential funding agency *want* to see it through.

Package the product with the "buyer" in mind: the grant applicant is asking the funding agency and probably also the local government (i.e., city council or board of supervisors) to "buy" a project proposal—to pay for services which will contribute to improvement of the criminal justice system in the community and in the state.

Illustratively it would be foolhardy to hire an individual who claimed he could provide technical assistance, for a fee, but could not explain just how. One would want that individual (just as the funding agency wants a grant applicant) to spell out clearly what assistance will ·be provided, how the work plan will be pursued, and why it is worth an investment of interest and financial support.

Place emphasis on the *need* and *value* of the results of the project. If it is necessary to educate the reader to the need, use the salesman's approach: To identify the need to sell a fire extinguisher to a man whose house is on fire without visible flame, fan the fire until the individual sees the flame and recognizes for himself the need and worth of the fire extinguisher. Do avoid use, however, of hard sell tactics. If the application is overloaded with justification, the reader will wonder about the tactics and sincerity of the applicant.

Another tip from business: It is easy to sell a customer something he wants to buy, if it is known what it is that he needs. One can sell a customer something he did not know he wanted, if one makes an attractive sales presentation. Occasionally one can sell a customer something he really does not want if it can be demonstrated why it is to his advantage to buy. *Know before a grant application is prepared whether the funding agency will be a willing, reluctant or resistant customer for the project concept.*

When assembling an application, rationalize how funding agencies pick from among competing applications. What things convince the funding agency to "buy" a project proposal? Use a strong merchandising approach in the preparation of an application.

Always keep in mind a few generalities typifying or conceptualizing funding agency evaluators:

- They are busy people.
- They have read a lot of other proposals and will not be fooled by "garbage".
- If a proposal makes a good or bad impression at the outset, that impression will probably prevail throughout the review process.
- They neither know your local area and situation nor do they want to become expert in these marginal details. They do know a lot about statewide and national problems and trends. Tailor the discussion of the problem accordingly.
- They are human beings, doing their jobs. They will be impressed by quality and by new ideas, bored by the tired and traditional. They will be tough judges, because they must answer to Congress. They want to help the applicant towards solution of a clearly articulated problem or problems: but the applicant also must help them to do their own jobs well.

A Few Suggestions To Keep On The Right Track

The fact that a police agency may "need' new uniforms, or weapons, or vehicles, or buildings simply because existing equipment is not good enough or new enough or big enough *does not* justify a grant. If it can be shown how such things, if acquired, will significantly reduce crime or improve public safety, *and do it better* than beefed up training programs, or reorganization, or other efforts where new staff and equipment are not needed or are of secondary concern, then the proposal has a good chance for approval.

Beware of hardware salesmen!

The fact that one city bought a particular piece of hardware does not mean that another city needs it, or that it will even work in the second situation. If one parrots a salesman's pitch in a grant application, it will fall on deaf ears!

Do not plan on funding resources for buildings

Why can't one achieve the same results by doing things differently, i.e. by modifying an existing building, or better yet, by changing practices and operations within existing facilities? Buildings offer no spin-off benefits for other areas; no one profits but the immediate local community, and sometimes that is hard to prove.

Do not take a "trust us" attitude

Some very thin applications say, in effect, "give us the money; we know what to do with it." Some very thick ones—usually prepared by systems consultants—seek to overpower the reader with sheer bulk and word power, so that the project proposal reviewers dare not question the proposed activity. The funding agency cannot afford to trust an applicant on blind faith. Project funding decisions must be defended to the federal government, which does not even accept the decisions of project approval authorities on blind faith.

Do not waste everyone's time.

If a project proponent cannot make a soundly conceived project presentation, or if the proponent has only a vague and undeveloped idea of project goals, do not try to fill out the forms. Frustration will be the inevitable reward. In the time it will take for an application to be rejected, the applicant could have been developing a concise and well-supported proposal. Remember that any funding agency will begin to doubt the capability of an applicant agency that submits an obviously weak and poorly thought out proposal.

Words, Words, Words: Find Someone Who Knows How To Write!

How long should the application be? What should be said, and what should not be said? How should the project proposal be structured? Use knowledge, training, common sense, and the following guidelines:

1. Say as much as necessary, and as little as possible. Anticipate questions, but do not burden the reader with unnecessary detail. If a key point can be summarized in 20 words instead of 200, do it.
2. Be clear, simple, direct, succinct. Easier said than done? Read some good newspaper articles and editorials. The men who wrote them are salesmen, just like the successful project applicant.
3. Look at the current advertisements that are selling products so well. The best are simple, short, direct, often with a big wallop or a new slant. Try it.
4. Get to the point immediately. The suspense approach of the mystery novel is out of place here. State immediately, in the summary, the objectives, the general approach, and the nature of the problem.
5. Use topic headings and subtitles in the text where appropriate. Use them where they will help the reader to follow the idea and to keep different ideas straight. Do not use them just to be doing it!
6. Avoid long sentences or paragraphs. Do not let a project proposal applicator get stuck in the mire and lose the point that the project applicant is trying to make.

7.   Avoid social science or systems "fluff" and jargon of any kind, including words that are only commonly used in the profession or in the community. Find more common terms for "interface," "phase-in," "phase-out," "meaningful," "dialogue," "coordinate," "tac squad," "narc squad," "2146 PC," "DWI," and similar expressions.

8.   Look out for the four most common language faults: marathon sentences, weak verbs, vague words, and unneeded words. A sentence should be 20-25 words long; dictating makes them shorter. Use verbs to convey action: "The city has built. . ." is better than "The city has completed construction of. . . ." or "Construction has been completed of. . ." What does this mean: "These effects will influence the expected results." Does it add anything to the argument?

Often the technical expert on the project is not the one best qualified to write the application

A team consisting of the top program man and the man with the best writing and sales abilities can work well. The writer will ask questions about points which are unclear, and which would very likely be unclear to project evaluators as well. A project applicant who is close to a project tends to assume that others know a lot more about it than they really do. The project applicant may work with a particular problem eight hours a day, whereas others may look at it for a few minutes or perhaps only as much as an hour a week.

The Forms Are Friends–Know And Respect Them

One should develop a respect, an understanding, and an appreciation of the application forms themselves as *powerful communications media and sales tools.* Businessmen use newspapers, television, billboards, radio, free offers, promotional gimmicks of all kinds to sell their wares. The project proponent has only a set of application forms, which must be backed up by all the personal contacts that can be exploited.

Forms are designed for a purpose. It will help the applicant to try to understand and further that purpose: The forms are intended to *help organize and present in a logical manner all the information which the funding agency needs to make and justify a funding decision.*

Perish the thought that the forms are just a medium of self-expression, or a kind of torture or obstacle course, or a game of Twenty Questions, or I've Got A Secret. They are designed to help the applicant, the project evaluator and others to measure the probable worth of a potential project. Use them to their best advantage.

If an applicant knows a project well, it should be relatively easy to provide a lot more information than the forms require. Remember the rule: say as much as necessary and as little as possible. Explain the need for the proposed project, and *convince the funding agency (and others) of the project's value* to the grantor and grantee, without losing, boring, or confusing the application evaluator.

Carefully Read and Follow the Instructions

Great pains often are taken to design a grant application form, only to find that those who use it seem to literally ignore the words in front of their eyes while filling it out. Have you ever asked someone his name, only to have him respond with his address? If so, it is easy enough to imagine how the application evaluator reacts when the work program is included under "objectives", when the title of the project is left out, when budget detail is under "project summary" or left out completely. This does not fool people; it only makes the grant applicant look stupid, unless there is some good (and stated) reason for deviating from the prescribed format.

All resource agency application forms will provide an accompanying set of instructions. In some cases, virtually every possible question or problem has been anticipated and the applicant is led by the hand through the preparation maze. Usually the funding agency has made the job so easy that the applicant probably does not deserve a grant if the prescribed forms are fouled up. *If there are questions, though, ASK.* Call the state or regional coordinator, or the field representatives, who are paid to help the grant applicant.

If trouble is experienced in filling in the blanks, most likely the applicant is working on the forms prematurely. More time should be spent on the basic proposal. Only in rare cases does the peculiar nature of a project not lend itself to the format of the application. If there simply is not room for a proper answer or explanation, attach separate pages, clearly identified with the project name and the item number to which they pertain. If a question or blank is not relevant to a specific project proposal presentation, write in "Does Not Apply". Master the forms and procedures, modifying only as absolutely necessary to strengthen the project proposal.

Stick to the basics: *where you are* (the problem and the need), *where you want to go* (the expected results), and *how you propose to get there* (plan or strategy, and the work program).

What A Resource Agency Looks For: A Few "Buypoints"

When an application is submitted, the project reviewers begin to look for certain key items—"buypoints"—that will influence them either to "buy" or to turn down a proposal.

Keep these points in mind when formulating a basic proposal, when writing an application, and in checking an application for completeness after it has been written and is ready for submission.

Few projects can encompass all of these points. Do not hesitate to amend the presentation if extra points can be picked up with a little extra effort. But likewise do not push a project proposal out of shape to accommodate things that really do not fit. Write in those "buypoints" which logically belong, and get as many in as are pertinent and reasonable. If an effort is made to cram in a lot of things that do not belong, the evaluators may be amused, but they will not be impressed—except perhaps negatively.

In many cases a "buypoint" can be incorporated into a single sentence or very short paragraph. In some cases "buypoints" simply emerge from the general nature and quality of the application. In all cases, be sure to include each item where it logically belongs in discussion of the project. A series of unrelated sentences, attempting to cover the list of buypoints, will look strange indeed, and will not contribute towards eventual project approval—but rather may contribute to disapproval.

The list of buypoints on the following pages are numbered for convenience, not necessarily for priority. They are, however, very generally arranged in order of importance. This is not an "official" checklist. It is based upon experience in working with funding agencies. Different agencies will place priority on different things. Some will pay no attention to certain of the points listed. This section is intended purely as an aid, offering some basic points to keep in mind when putting together a grant proposal and final application.

1. *Conformity With The Act and With State and Regional Plans.*
   The project must conform with the intent and priorities of the basic legislation and with state and regional comprehensive plans. Check this before doing anything else, and be prepared to fight if the project does not clearly conform to legislative criteria.

2. *Capability of Agency.*
   The funding agency must be satisfied that the applicant agency is capable of carrying out the proposed project. Merely saying so will not help. The applicant agency must prove it by the quality of the application submitted, the qualifications of its people, local support for the project concept, past performance on other projects, and the overall financial situation. The type of project proposed must logically relate to the type of agency submitting the proposal (e.g., drug abuse control and Health Department). Private, non-profit organizations must take special care to demonstrate their capabilities.

3. *Problems To Be Solved Is Clearly Defined, Localized, And Of Manageable Dimensions.*
   If the project application does not clearly define the

problem which requires a solution, it will be difficult if not impossible to determine the effectiveness of measures designed to solve it. State the problem, in quantitative terms if possible. Outline different factors or aspects of the problem. Identify those factors which the project expects to influence or control, those which it cannot control, and the possible effects of the latter in diluting the prospects for project success.

Be realistic! Define the scope of the problem in manageable terms. Do not expect to accomplish the impossible—because in the end this will only minimize project success and exaggerate failures.

Be knowledgeable concerning project dimensions and the relation of project parameters to larger issues.

Be sure that the proposed solution is within the realm of probable realization, and that it bears directly upon essential project goals and objectives.

Localize the description of the problem. State and national statistics can be used to introduce local figures, to show the larger impact of specific project activities, and to show conformity with the state plan and the Act. But the project presentation must use local numbers to describe the problem, as it exists, as the proponent understands it in the community, and to show what effect the project will have on the problem. It must be shown that the numbers are meaningful and reliable. Evaluation of the activity will be mostly an analysis of what actual project performance has done or will do to change these local numbers.

4. *Objectives Clear and Measurable.*
Nothing is more important to any project than the end product. This is what is being sold to the funding agency and what they are paying for. There must be a clear definition of what the project will deliver, how results will be accomplished, and how it will be known when the delivery has been made (evaluation). When staff has been hired, equipment pur-

chased, and operations have gotten underway, money will have been spent—but the product will not necessarily have been delivered. The product must be a measurable improvement in law enforcement, public safety, or in diminution of the level of crime. "To hire five special officers for walking patrol in the business district" is not objective. "To reduce the incidence of theft and street crimes by 20% in the business district over a twelve month period" is a demonstrably measureable objective—what the project hopes to achieve by hiring the new officers. In the case of certain serious problems, the objective may be simply to hold the line: to keep the problems from getting worse. This also is measureable. If the project proponent cannot seem to attach measurable units to stated objectives, keep refining them until measureable units do prevail. If objectives are too general, and results cannot be measured (even by "non-scientific", impressionistic means), then the chances of knowing what has been accomplished when the project is done are slim—and so are the chances of further funding. The units of measurement should be established in advance: crime rates, response time, rates of recidivism, processing time, changed attitudes (based upon surveys). If there is clearly no way to adequately measure results, say so in advance, while simultaneously explaining why the project is nonetheless important, and how it is proposed to evaluate results in the absence of finite measurement.

. *Evaluation Component Fully Described and Sound.*
The planned method for evaluating the results of project work must be an integral part of any proposal. A funding agency's requirements in this regard are spelled out in their application instructions. The evaluators' assessment of the proposal will weigh heavily upon the adequacy and soundness of the evaluation plan, since the funding agency must later be able to judge, in as concrete terms as possible, whether its investment has paid off in terms of com-

munity benefit. Evaluation is simply the comparison of accomplishments with objectives, and it is simple if both roject objectives and a means of measuring accomplishment have been carefully defined.

6. *Detailed Work Program.* The funding agency wants to know exactly what tasks will be performed, by whom, and the man-hours required for completion of each one. This will demonstrate management capability, and also will help to keep all the pieces together throughout the project period.

   A project proponent will never know whether an approach to solving a problem was valid, unless the project adheres to a pre-designed work program, logically organized to take one from the problem to the final solution. Too many projects fail because in the last month somebody suddenly realizes that everyone has been extremely busy, and most of the money has been spent, but no one is sure just what everyone has been doing, and how their individual and separate activities relate to the accomplishment of the basic objectives.

   A complete work schedule (sometimes handled well by using PERT) can help to correct difficulties as they arise, and keep the project moving ahead on a pre-determined time-phased basis.

7. *Qualified Staff Will Conduct the Project.*
   A project (like an organization) will rise or fall on the abilities of the people running it. The funding agency wants to know who they are, why they are qualified to do the job, how much time they will spend on it, and exactly what they will contribute toward accomplishment of project objectives. Do not attach resumes of top people to an application unless the named individuals are prepared to commit a good deal of their time to the project. This would be deceptive, the funding agency will see through it, and it will not help get the job done.

   By all means, nominate the best qualified persons available to staff a specific project. A clear willingness to commit good people can make the difference between funding and non-funding. If staff is to be recruited from outside sources, the capabilities of such individuals must be spelled out as thoroughly as those of permanent staff.

8. *Innovation.*

   If the project proponent is doing something different, or doing something common differently, or approaching a problem that has never been tackled (successfully) before, the proposal is probably meritorious. Sometimes the "innovative" aspects of a project can save it if funding is doubtful on the basis of its other merits. Talk to people. There are a lot of new ideas around. Do not be afraid to try them.

9. *Evidence That Other Alternatives Were Explored.*

   Why did the project proponent choose the proposed method or solution out of the range of possibilities? Briefly outline other alternatives that were considered, and the reasons for rejecting them. Anticipate the inevitable question: "Couldn't the same thing be accomplished better or more cheaply by other means?"

10. *Evidence That Prior Research Has Been Studied.*

    Demonstrate, by giving specific references, that other authorities have been consulted in the general and specific problem areas with which the project proposal is concerned, that pertinent studies or reports have been read, that other communities or agencies with similar problems have been contacted, and that there is general awareness of how the proposed efforts will fit into the total picture of the work being done elsewhere in the particular problem area.

11. *Inter-Agency Cooperation.*

    It always is to a project proponent's advantage to contact any and all agencies, organizations or groups in the community who have a potential interest in the proposed project. This will ensure a good atmosphere for the project, and save much discontent later.

    Indicate in the proposal which groups were contacted and the nature of their reactions.

Far better both from the project proponent's point of view and the funding source are commitments of cooperation from other groups. Projects conducted jointly by more than one city, county, or agency make federal money go farther. If joint sponsorship is not in order, get letters from other agencies and groups, in which they pledge time, money, people, or other concrete support to the project. It costs little, and means little, for any agency or group to promise only "cooperation".

12. *Tie-In With Other Programs.*

There are bound to be other programs in the community, region, or in the state which are related to what is being proposed, some of them possibly assisted by the same funding source. Show *at least* an awareness of these similar activities. Better yet, explain some logical relationship between recommended new activities and others which are either planned or actually are underway. If possible, find some way in which the proposed project can work collaboratively with another. Try to show (in not too many words) that the project not only will not be in conflict with others, but that in some way it will complement, supplement, or be supportive of others. This is particularly important in areas of training, drugs and alcoholism, juvenile delinquency, civil disorder control, and communications.

13. *Impact On The Total Criminal Justice System.*

In the eyes of the funding agency, a good project should be able to demonstrate some direct relationship between expected results and some improvement in the total criminal justice system, either locally or at the state or national level. This is particularly likely to happen where the project is innovative, trying something new, something which could have application elsewhere if it succeeds. Also the application might show how a police, or court, or probation, or health program will have an impact on other elements of the system: Fewer drug users means fewer arrests fewer court cases, less burden on the probation departments, etc.

14. *Maximum Use of All Available Funds.*

    Many funding agencies say "no" by suggesting that the funding applicant knock on all other doors before coming to them. Do this in advance. Funding agencies like to see the creative use of available financial resources, and chances of support from one agency are good if there already is some prospect of support from others. If a joint funding package cannot be put together, at least explain that other sources were explored and that the instant application represents the last resort.

15. *Availability of Local Share.*

    It must be shown, unequivocally, that the applicant understands the concept of federal (or state)—local partnership, and that the necessary local share of the funding in man-hours, services, materials, or cold cash is pledged. Remember that the ability to commit the local share may require action by the City Council or Board of Supervisors, and perhaps modifications in the applicant agency's basic budget. Get all of this done ahead of time, before the project application is submitted to the funding agency.

16. *Intention To Assume Future Costs.*

    Most grants are intended to be "seed money"—to help get something going which later will be supported entirely with local funds. A statement recognizing this fact, and committing the community or agency to future financial support of the project (if possible) is important.

17. *Reasonable and Detailed Budget.*

    If the proposal is soundly developed, the budget should not be a big problem. Evaluators will look first at the substantive aspects of the application—the concept, the approach, the people; then they will study the budget. If the applicant has spent the necessary effort doing a good selling job on the basic project concept, chances are the evaluators will be somewhat more flexible with respect to the budget. A *perfectly costed poor proposal does no good.* A good proposal at least opens the door, so the budget can be negotiated if necessary. However, the budget will be checked for reasonableness and accuracy. Here are some basic guidelines to help the applicant through the budget maze.

a. Include the necessary, but no more.
b. Work back and forth from the detailed work program to the budget.
c. Provide reasonable amounts for inflation, salary increases, etc., but do not consciously pad.
d. Check federal limitations on expenditure items (Office of Management and Budget Circular A-87) *before* writing them into the budget.
e. Add, subtract, multiply, and divide correctly.
f. Be sure that the proper matching formula has been applied to the project.
g. Get help in making cost estimates from purchasing and personnel staffs, utility companies, realtors, agencies that have had similar programs, etc.
h. Explain the basis for all cost estimates (e.g., 6 mos. @ $175/mo = $1050.00).
i. Be sure that each item of expenditure can be justified in terms of the requirements of the work program.

To arrive at a "balanced" budget, it probably will be necessary to work back and forth from the estimates of project costs to the available local funds, and how much the project might get from the funding agency and other non-local sources. A good budget, carefully documenting each line item should include the following:

a. Personnel
   Salaries
   Fringe Benefits

b. Consultants and Consultant Services
Legal
Accounting
Professional
c. Travel
Local, statewide, etc.
Costs per mile based on either local policy or federal guidelines.
d. Equipment (check policy of funding source on this item before including)
Office
Programmatic
e. Operating expenses and supplies
Consumables
Rental and/or facility costs
Phone
Utilities
Postage
f. Special Project Costs
Any costs specific to the program; for example, meals served in a drug treatment center, printing original materials, equipment rental. Check policy of funding source. Often these expenses may be included under the category of supplies and operating expenses.
g. Indirect costs (if allowable) A percentage of the total grant request charged for overhead. If allowed, the funding agency will have specific policies and guidelines concerning indirect costs.
h. Local contributions
Some funding agencies require a percentage of matching funds and/or in-kind contributions. Reflect these matching funds and in-kind contributions in the budget.
18. *Urgency and Importance To The Applicant.*
Presumably grant applications are not filed for the fun of it, although some people file them simply because there is money available. A funding agency

wants to know just how important, how urgent the proposed project is to any community or area. What other things hinge on completion of the project?

What could happen if the project were delayed? Make the case appropriately strong, but do not exaggerate; be brief.

19. *Internal Consistency of the Application.* Each section of an application should logically flow into the next, and all should clearly be part of a larger concept and idea. Be consistent in the use of terms and numbers. This is no problem if the project proposal has been carefully considered and outlined before beginning to complete the forms.

20. *Compliance With Application Instructions.*
See earlier discussion.

21. *Clear, Direct, Simple, and Correct English.*
See earlier discussion.

22. *Maps, Charts, Tables.*
Always include a map of the area that will be served by the project. Include also any charts and tables which are *necessary* to explain or support the proposal or the need for the project. *Do not* include complex or elaborate charts and tables which might be only marginally "interesting" or "helpful". The evaluators will think they are extraneous and will not bother to read them.

All references and data should be relevant, *presented in a form which is easily used and understood,* and it should be drawn from reputable and *identified* sources. Techniques such as bar charts, use of color, overlays, etc. are fine if they actually help to make important data better understood.

23. *Physical Appearance.*
Mailing an application to a funding agency is the equivalent of submitting a request on behalf of the county, or the courthouse, or city hall, or the sponsoring agency, and/or the community. Thus it is absolutely essential that the original project submission make a good impression. A messy, unattractive application suggests that the proponent, the sponsor-

ing agency, and the community does not care much about the project, and that the proponent may not have the necessary talent to carry it forward to successful completion.

24. *Project Title*

Give the project a short title, one which clearly explains the purpose of the project. Cute, pompous, mysterious, and oddball titles can confuse the public, and others not directly familiar with the project. Acronyms (CLETS, SWAT, CNIN) are often in vogue, but using such terms tells the reader or listener nothing about the project and its importance to the community.

25. *Submission Procedures*

Submission procedures may vary considerably among funding agencies. Be very sure to check the guidelines, or consult with the funding agency staff, particularly concerning:

a. Deadlines. Are the deadlines based on postmark or receipt date? If a deadline becomes critical, send the original copy via the quickest means possible, i.e. first class, and request a receipt be returned by the post office. Any additional copies required may be mailed by a less costly means.

b. Number of copies: The number of copies required of a grant application may vary from one to twenty or thirty. Always be aware of the precise number required.

There is one other possibility that should be considered. In the case where a federal agency is the funding source, check on any requirements for simultaneous submission to any state or local agency. The funding agency staff should be able to advise concerning the existence of any such requirement.

26. *Additional Technical Requirements Imposed.*

There are several additional requirements that are imposed upon the project proponent besides completing the application. All of the following are federal requirements. Funding agency staff should be familiar with these requirements and can be of assistance in complying with them.

    a.   Office of Management and Budget (OMB) Circular A-95

    b.   Equal Employment Opportunity Certification.

    c.   Environmental Impact Requirements.

OMB Circular A-95

Briefly described, the OMB Circular A-95 is a pre-application review and grant notification procedure. The intent of A-95 is to promote more effective coordination of planning and development activities carried on or assisted by the federal government.

    The major device of A-95 is encouragement of systematic communications between the federal government, and state, and local governments carrying out these related planning and development activities. The following is a list of major program areas requiring compliance with the A-95 Review procedure. This list is not necessarily exclusive of other program areas.

- HUD: Comprehensive planning (701) program.
- DOT: Urban highway planning; mass transportation planning; airport systems planning.
- EPA: Water quality management planning; air pollution control planning; solid waste planning.
- HEW: Comprehensive health planning (314b); planning for the aged.
- DOL: Areawide manpower planning.
- USDA: Resource conservation and development planning.
- OEO: Community action planning.
- EDA: Economic development district planning.
- ARC: Local development district planning.
- LEAA: Law Enforcement planning.

Equal Employment Opportunity Commission

On March 9, 1973 the Law Enforcement Association Administration of the Department of Justice (LEAA), promulgated equal employment opportunity guidelines (28CFR 42.301, et seq, subpart E), as a consequence of Title VII of the Civil Rights Act of 1064 (42 U.S.C. par. 2000 e) as amended by the Equal Employment Opportunity Act of March 24, 1972, Public Law No. 92-261. The 1972 amendments to the 1964 Act made two significant changes to Title VII by:

1. providing for creation of the U.S. Equal Employment Opportunity Commission (EEOC), the agency empowered to administer the law. The authority to enforce its provisions in federal court; and

2. extending EEOC's jurisdiction to include public employees with 25 or more employees as well as private employees; the U.S. Attorney General presently has the power to enforce the prohibitions concerning public employees, and this power was transferred to EEOC on March 24, 1974.

Funding agencies will be able to provide these guidelines. Be cognizant of these regulations and their limitations, and determine whether or not the applicant agency/department must comply, or meet any of the exemption criteria.

Environmental Impact Requirements

Determine what procedure the funding agency requires in complying with environmental impact requirements. Again, funding agency staff can be of assistance both in understanding the requirements and in preparation of the documentation. Funding agency environmental procedures and requirements will be based on the provisions of the National Environmental Policy Act, NEPA, (42 USCA 4321 et seq.), the National Historic Preservation Act (16 USCA 470 et seq.), the policies adoped by the federal funding agency, the guidelines issued by the Council on Environmental Quality, CEQ, (36 CFR 7724-7729) and any state act and administrative code.

The "Completed" Application

When the grant application has been completed and appears to be ready for actual submission, it would be wise to have a critical pre-submission review by someone who is familiar with the general project concept. This independent reading by a friendly critic may result in last minute suggestions for minor modification and improvement of the grant application request. Criticism concerning content and style should be taken seriously, since the friendly critic may have a viewpoint closely paralleling that of the individuals who will render final judgment on the proposal at the local, regional and state levels.

Also invite the ultimate critics to comment. Submit a draft to the Regional Coordinator, and/or to the field representatives. These individuals will comment honestly and with knowledge and experience, thus saving the grant applicant a lot of time later.

Check, once again, to be sure that the application does conform with prescribed submission procedures. Do not compromise chances for approval by trying to circumvent those people charged with responsibility for ultimate evaluation of the proposal.

If possible, make a personal appearance before the State or Regional Advisory Board, when the project is under active consideration. Even when the best possible job has been done in preparing an application, people still manage to come up with questions that were not anticipated during the course of writing up the grant request.

If, after the completion of much arduous work the project proposal gets tabled or rejected, and the applicant still is convinced that it is worthy of support, initiate an appeal. There are formal appeal procedures. If the applicant questions either state or regional priorities and procedures, efforts should be made to get them changed. Do not give up too soon, defeated by the bureaucracy. Always remember that a grant applicant is dealing with people, whose ideas change or can be changed. These individuals usually are honestly willing to collaborate if the grant applicant exhibits a genuine desire to work cooperatively to improve the project concept and prospects for the realistic achievement of stated objectives. Since nothing is certain in this or any other game, one last word—Good Luck!

REFERENCES

A Guide For Successful Proposal Development, Chicago: Funding Sources Clearinghouse, Inc., 1973. A good description of grant application development process.

Cain, Robert D. Jr., Director, National Council on Crime and Delinquency, "The Juvenile Justice and Delinquency Prevention Act of 1974," Tucson, Arizona: *Soundings,* Vol. 2, No. 3, May-June, 1975. Reviews in detail the key factors in the Juvenile Justice and Delinquency Prevention Act.

Catalog of Federal Domestic Assistance, Executive Office of the President, Office of Management and Budget, Washington, D. C.: Government Printing Office, 1975. Lists all Federal Domestic Assistance programs. A must for the planner responsible for grant preparation.

Crime Control Act of 1973. Public Law 93-83, 93rd Congress, H. R. 8152, August 6, 1975. The Act describes the purpose and function of the Law Enforcement Assistance Administration.

Workshop On Application of grant application development process, California Council on Criminal Justice, Region M., 1970. A good description of grant application development. Emphasis is on procedural techniques to grant preparation.

NATIONAL ADVISORY COMMISSION REPORTS ON STANDARDS AND GOALS FOR CRIMINAL JUSTICE, *CRIMINAL JUSTICE SYSTEMS*, WASHINGTON, 1973, pp. 1-7.

REPORT REFERENCE AND SYNOPSIS

Standards:
1.1 Assure that criminal justice planning is crime-oriented.
1.2 Improve the linkage between criminal justice planning and budgeting.
1.3 Set minimum statewide standards for recipients of criminal justice grants and subgrants.
1.4 Develop criminal justice planning capabilities.
1.5 Encourage the participation of operating agencies and the public in the criminal justice planning process.

Recommendation:
1.1 Urge the federal government to apply these standards in its own planning.

Standards:
3.1 Coordinate the development of criminal justice information systems and make maximum use of collected data.
3.2 Establish a State criminal justice information system that provides certain services.
3.3 Provide localities with information systems that support the needs of local criminal justice agencies.
3.4 Provide every component of the criminal justice system with an information system that supports interagency needs.

Standards:

4.1 Define the proper function of a police information system.
4.2 Utilize information to improve the department's crime analysis capability.
4.3 Develop a police manpower resource allocation and control system.
4.4 Specify maximum allowable delay for information delivery.
4.5 Insure that all police agencies participate in the Uniform Crime Report program.
4.6 Expand collection of crime data.
4.7 Insure quality control of crime data.
4.8 Establish a geocoding system for crime analysis.

Standards:

5.1 Provide background data and case history for criminal justice decision making.
5.2 Provide information on caseflow to permit efficient calendar management.
5.3 Provide capability to determine monthly criminal justice caseflow and workloads.
5.4 Provide data to support charge determination and case handling.
5.5 Create capability for continued research and evaluation.
5.6 Record action taken in regard to one individual and one distinct offense and record the number of criminal events.

Standards:

6.1 Define the needs of a corrections information system.
6.2 Apply uniform definitions to all like correctional data.
6.3 Design a corrections data base that is flexible enough to allow for expansion.
6.4 Collect certain data about the offender.

6.5 Account for offender population and movement.
6.6 Describe the corrections experience of the offender.
6.7 Evaluate the performance of the corrections system.

Standards:
7.1 Provide for compatible design of offender-based transaction statistics and computerized criminal history systems.
7.2 Develop single data collection procedures for offender-based transaction statistics and computerized criminal history systems.
7.3 Develop data bases simultaneously for offender-based transaction statistics and computerized criminal history systems.
7.4 Restrict dissemination of criminal justice information.
7.5 Insure completeness and accuracy of offender data.
7.6 Safeguard systems containing criminal offender data.
7.7 Establish computer interfaces for criminal justice information systems.
7.8 Insure availability of criminal justice information systems.

Standards:
8.1 Insure the privacy and security of criminal justice information systems.
8.2 Define the scope of criminal justice information systems files.
8.3 Limit access and dissemination of criminal justice information.
8.4 Guarantee the right of the individual to review information in criminal justice information systems relating to him.
8.5 Adopt a system of classifying criminal justice system data.

8.6 Protect criminal justice information from environmental hazards.

8.7 Implement a personnel clearance system.

8.8 Establish criteria for the use of criminal justice information for research.

8.9 Establish criteria for the use of criminal justice information for research.

Standards:

9.1 Insure standardized terminology following the National Crime Information Center example.

9.2 Establish specific program language requirements for criminal justice information systems.

9.3 Assure adequate teleprocessing capability.

Standards:

10.1 Take legislative actions to support the development of criminal justice information systems.

10.2 Establish criminal justice user groups.

10.3 Establish a plan for development of criminal justice information and statistics systems at state and local levels.

10.4 Consolidate services to provide criminal justice information support where it is not otherwise economically feasible.

10.5 Require conformity with all standards of this report as a condition for grant approval.

Standards:

11.1 Monitor the criminal justice information system analysis, design, development, and initial steps leading to implementation.

11.2 Monitor the implementation of the system to determine the cost and performance of the system and its component parts.

11.3 Conduct evaluations to determine the effectiveness of information system components.

Standards:

12.1 Develop, implement, and evaluate criminal justice education and training programs.

12.2 Establish criminal justice system curricula.

Standards:

13.1 Revise criminal codes in states where codes have not been revised in the past decade.

13.2 Complete revision of criminal codes.

13.3 Simplify the penalty structure in criminal codes.

13.4 Revise corrections laws.

13.5 Create a drafting body to carry out criminal code revision.

13.6 Revise criminal procedure laws.

13.7 Support drafted criminal law legislation with interpretative commentaries.

13.8 Assure smooth transition to the new law through education.

13.9 Continue law revision efforts through a permanent commission.

INDEX

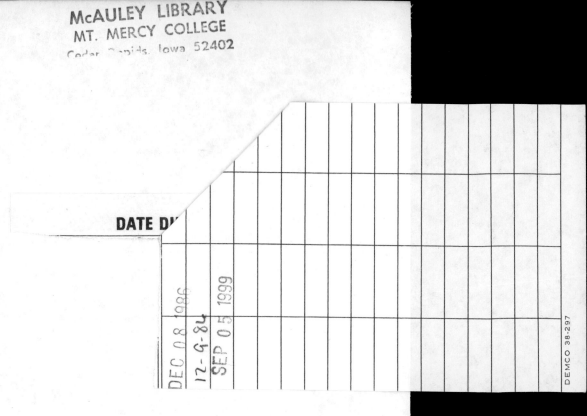